PROFESSIONAL STUDIO TECHNIQUES
DESIGN ESSENTIALS

Luanne Seymour Cohen ▪ Tanya Wendling

D1538180

Adobe Press
Mountain View, California

Library of Congress Catalog No.: 94-76914

ISBN: 1-56830-093-x

10 9 8 7 6 5 4 3 2   First Printing: January 1995

Published and distributed to the trade by Hayden Books, a division of Macmillan Computer Publishing. For information, address Hayden Books, 201 w. 103 Street, Indianapolis, IN 46290. For corporate, educational, or individual sales information, call Macmillan Computer Publishing 800-428-5331 or 317-581-3500.

Credits

Authors: Luanne S. Cohen, Tanya Wendling

Book Design/Art Director: Lisa Jeans

Cover Design: Eric Baker

Cover Illustration: Louis Fishauf

Illustration: Hung Yin-Yin

Other Contributors: Patrick Ames, Rita Amladi, David Biedny, Russell Brown, Don Cutbirth, Joan Delfino, Laura Dower, Mikyong Han, Kim Isola, Julieanne Kost, Bert Monroy, Jim Ryan, Karen Tenenbaum, Judy Walthers von Alten, James Young

Photographers: Artbeats (pp. 60, 70, 76), CMCD (pp. 38, 80), Luanne S. Cohen (pp. 15, 32, 39, 67, 78), Digital Stock (pp. 14, 26, 32, 40, 54, 56, 57, 66, 74, 80), Disc Imagery (p. 68), D'Pix Folio 1 (p. 38), Curtis Fukuda (p. 84), Lisa Jeans (p. 74), Julieanne Kost (pp. 26, 40), Doug Menuez (p. 92), Form and Function (p. 22), PhotoDisc (pp. 24, 26, 34, 38, 54, 74, 84), Stock Options (p. 38)

Contents

Introduction

Design Essentials, Second Edition shows how to produce traditional graphic and photographic effects using Adobe Illustrator™ and Adobe Photoshop™ software. This book, like the books in the Professional Studio Techniques series, does not attempt to describe the features of the Adobe software programs. Instead it is a quick how-to reference for artists familiar with the basic tools and commands in the programs.

The techniques included in *Design Essentials, Second Edition* were collected and developed over the course of a year; many people—both within and outside of Adobe Systems—have contributed to the book. Each procedure has been tested extensively and each piece of sample art has been proofed on a variety of printers and imagesetters. *Design Essentials, Second Edition* also includes numerous tips on working efficiently with Adobe software. These tips are marked with the ∾ symbol throughout the book.

Design Essentials, Second Edition covers the most recent versions of the Adobe software: Adobe Photoshop 3.0, running on Macintosh® and Windows™, and Adobe Illustrator 5.5, running on Macintosh and UNIX®. In addition, many of the techniques in this book can be reproduced using earlier versions of the software. The required software for each technique is indicated beneath the technique title. Where Macintosh and Windows versions of a software program may be used, keyboard shortcuts for both versions are provided using the following format:

⌘/Ctrl = ⌘ (Macintosh) or Ctrl (Windows)
Option/Alt = Option (Macintosh) or Alt (Windows)

For the keyboard shortcuts for the different UNIX environments, please see the Quick Reference Card that came with your software or refer to your documentation.

1 Working Efficiently

Designing with production in mind

Setting up your system

Working efficiently in Adobe Illustrator

Working efficiently in Adobe Photoshop

Working efficiently

The time it takes to open or save a file, send a file to the printer, or refresh the screen after performing an operation is a measure of a program's "performance." While performance is in part determined by the type of computer and the amount of computer memory you have, many other factors affect performance dramatically. These factors include how you have set up your software, the size of your file, the complexity of the file, and how you perform certain tasks. This section provides guidelines for improving performance and for minimizing the size and complexity of your files. It also provides workarounds for working with large and complex files and general tips for working efficiently in both Adobe Photoshop and Adobe Illustrator.

Designing with production in mind

An important part of a successful design project is making sure that the project can be produced on the equipment available and within the constraints of the schedule and budget. Often a design ends up requiring multiple proofs and reworkings that could have been avoided by planning for production at the outset of the project. Finding out how a project will be produced will help you make design decisions up front that will save you time, money, and frustration at the end of the project.

Determine print specifications. Work with your printer to define resolution and line screen, paper stock, or special printing needs such as varnishes or custom inks. These factors can affect both the design of your artwork and how you set up the file. For example, the line screen and resolution you will use determine the best way to set up blends in Adobe Illustrator (see page 42) as well as the image size and resolution you can use in Adobe Photoshop.

Calibrate your system. Both Adobe Photoshop and Adobe Illustrator include features for calibrating your color monitor to help ensure that the color you see on-screen is as close a match as possible to the color you see in your printed output. In addition, Photoshop contains a set of dialog boxes for calibrating the software for different printing environments. Follow the step-by-step instructions in the user guides to calibrate your system.

Create file-information documents. Like most page-layout programs, Adobe Photoshop 3.0 and later and Adobe Illustrator 5.5 and later let you track characteristics of a job in a separate file that can be kept with your document files (called File Info in Photoshop and Document Info in Illustrator). Information such as photographer, legal rights, scanning resolution, and fonts used can be included in these files for easy reference. Check your user guides for details.

Setting up your system

The way you set up your system can dramatically affect performance. Macintosh® System 7™ and Microsoft® Windows™ 3.1 both have the capability of using *virtual memory*—hard disk space that can be used for temporary storage of data when physical random access memory (RAM) is insufficient. In addition, Adobe Photoshop has its own version of virtual memory called the *scratch disk*. The drawback of virtual memory is that it takes significantly more time to read and write files using virtual memory disk space than using physical RAM. For this reason, the best way to improve performance with large files is to increase the amount of RAM allocated to Photoshop.

An easy way to find out whether you're using virtual memory in Adobe Photoshop is to select the small triangle at the bottom left of the document window and choose Scratch Sizes from the pop-up menu. The number on the left is the amount of memory taken up by all open windows and the Clipboard; the number on the right is the total amount of RAM available. When the number on the left exceeds the number on the right, Photoshop begins using virtual memory.

Increase the memory allocation. If you are using a Macintosh, increase the amount of memory allocated to the application using the Info window. (To open the Info window, quit the application, select its icon in the Finder, and choose File > Get Info.) If you are using System 7 on a non-Power Macintosh, and you have more than 8 MB of RAM, turn on 32-bit addressing in the Memory control panel before increasing the memory allocation above 8 MB. With Adobe Photoshop, always set the disk cache in the Memory control panel to its lowest setting.

Note that the Macintosh Quadra lets you set up a RAM disk. The RAM disk sets aside RAM for launching applications, but does not improve performance within applications. To improve performance in an application turn off the RAM disk and increase the memory allocated to the application.

Take full advantage of virtual memory in Adobe Photoshop. If you have more than one hard disk drive, choose File > Preferences > Scratch Disks in Adobe Photoshop, and assign the scratch disk to your fastest disk drive. Make sure that the amount of free space on the drive is greater than or equal to the amount of RAM you have allocated to Photoshop (on the Macintosh) or the amount of installed RAM (with Windows).

On the Macintosh, make sure that Apple's virtual memory is turned off in the Memory control panel. With Windows, double-click the 386 Enhanced icon in the Windows Control Panel, and set up the virtual memory so that it is equal to the amount of installed RAM.

If performance still seems slow, try optimizing the disk using a utility such as Norton Utilities™ or SUM™ (for the Macintosh) or Norton Utilities for Windows. If you are running DOS® version 6.0 or later, type **defrag** at the C: prompt, which automatically optimizes your disk.

Increase the size of the Adobe Type Manager™ font cache. If you're working with a file that contains type, you can significantly speed up processing by increasing the size of the font cache in the Adobe Type Manager (ATM™) control panel. A larger font cache lets you store more font sizes in memory so that ATM doesn't have to rebuild them each time the screen is redrawn. It also enables ATM to generate large sizes that would otherwise display as jagged characters. A font cache setting of 320K is sufficient for most projects.

Manage your fonts. On a Macintosh, use a font-management utility such as Suitcase™ to create and manage font suitcases. Because ATM can generate any size typeface from a single font size, be sure to store in your suitcase only the sizes you use most often for each type style—usually, 10 points or 12 points for body text, and 36 points or 48 points for display type. With Windows, you can use FontMinder™ to manage your fonts.

Keep the Clipboard clear of large amounts of data. Images and objects on the Clipboard are stored in RAM and so can significantly affect performance. To clear the Clipboard of large amounts of data, select a small area of the image you have open and copy the selection to replace the older Clipboard data. If you are working with Photoshop and another application, and you're not copying Photoshop data into the other application, deselect the Export Clipboard option in the More Preferences dialog box (choose File > Preferences > General, and then click More). This prevents Photoshop from exporting the Clipboard data every time you switch applications.

Turn off thumbnails and 2.5 compatibility. You may improve performance in Adobe Photoshop by turning off thumbnail previews both in the More Preferences dialog box and in the Layers and Channels palettes. (Make sure that the Full Size preview option in the More Preferences dialog box is also turned off.) Also, if you're working with layers and you don't need to save a flattened version of each file, deselect the 2.5 Format Compatibility option in the More Preferences dialog box. This option saves a non-layered version of the layered file and so may significantly increase the file size.

Optimize your components. The charts on the facing page show optimal hardware systems for two types of work environments. If you're not in the market for a completely new system, however, you can upgrade your equipment with any of the following components:

CPU upgrade boards. If possible, consider adding a current-model central processing unit (CPU) upgrade board to improve overall performance.

Accelerator cards. If you can't upgrade your CPU, talk to your hardware vendor about adding an accelerator card. Some accelerator cards boost overall CPU performance; others dramatically increase the redraw speed of graphics applications.

RAM. Install as much RAM as possible in the form of noncomposite SIMMs.

External hard disk drives. Find a drive that gives you adequate storage space and good throughput performance.

File transfer devices. If you transport large files often, consider removable cartridges or optical media.

RECOMMENDATIONS FOR DESIGN AND LAYOUT			
COMPONENT	MAC	POWER MAC	WINDOWS
CPU	QUADRA 650–950	7100/66 8100/80	486/PENTIUM
RAM	32 MB+	64 MB+	32 MB+
VIDEO CARD/ MONITOR	24-BIT/21″	24-BIT/21″	24-BIT/21″
HARD DISK DRIVE	500 MB–1 GB+	1 GB+	1 GB+

RECOMMENDATIONS FOR HIGH-END IMAGE PROCESSING			
COMPONENT	MAC	POWER MAC	WINDOWS
CPU	QUADRA 950	8100/80	PENTIUM
RAM	256 MB	256 MB	256 MB
VIDEO CARD/ MONITOR	24-BIT/21″	24-BIT/21″	24-BIT/21″
HARD DISK DRIVE	2 GB+	2 GB+	2 GB+

The type of system you need depends on your work environment. The charts here provide recommendations for two types of work environments: the top chart for creative work that doesn't require extensive processing of high-resolution images; the bottom chart for high-end prepress work and production. All of these recommended systems provide optimal performance for processing, display, and file transfer. Note that if you are using Windows NT, you can also take advantage of Intel-based machines with multiprocessors, which significantly boost the performance of Adobe Photoshop.

Working efficiently in Adobe Illustrator

Because the results of most Adobe Illustrator operations are displayed only in Preview mode, most performance issues for Illustrator are directly related to previewing artwork. Once you have set up your system for maximum efficiency, you can minimize the time it takes to preview and print by simplifying your files and by working around complex paths and images whenever possible.

Preview selectively. If your file is large or complex, you can dramatically speed up previewing either by using the Preview Selection command to preview selected objects only (⌘-Option+Y on the Macintosh; Ctrl+Y with Windows). You can also use the Layers palette in Illustrator 5.0 and later to preview objects on selected layers.

Work with two windows open. You can avoid having to switch back and forth between two views of an illustration by working with two windows open. For example, if you've magnified an image for detail work, choose Window > New Window and display the image at full size in the second window to monitor the effects of your changes. You can also use a second window to display an image in Preview mode while you work in the first window in Artwork mode.

Create custom views. In Adobe Illustrator 5.0 and later, you can use the New View command in the View menu to create custom views of your document. This feature is especially useful when you're working on several parts of a large document. Once you have created your custom views, use ⌘+Control+Number key (1–0) to quickly switch from view to view.

Preview without patterns. When possible, turn off the Preview and Print Patterns option in the Document Setup dialog box. Remember to turn the option back on before you print. (For a slight performance improvement in Artwork mode only, you can also deselect Show Placed Images.)

On the Macintosh, use ⌘-period to cancel previewing. In many cases, a partial preview gives you the information you need to continue with your work. Once Illustrator starts to redraw the screen in Preview mode, you can cancel at any time to return immediately to Artwork mode.

Delete unused patterns and custom colors. In general, it's good practice to delete any patterns and custom colors you are no longer using before you save or print the file. To do this, open the Patterns or Custom Color dialog box, click Select All Unused, and click Delete. Because the program deletes all patterns or custom colors used in all open files, make sure that you've closed all other files before performing this operation.

Simplify paths. Complex paths—including masks, compound paths, and paths with many anchor points—can slow processing and cause printing problems. You can simplify paths by deleting anchor points or by increasing flatness. Flatness determines the length, in pixels, of the straight-line segments used to approximate a curve. The higher the flatness, the less accurate the curve but the faster the printing. In Adobe Illustrator version 5.0 or later, you increase flatness for individual objects by decreasing the Output Resolution value for the objects in the Attributes dialog box. See the user guide for details.

Split paths. Another way to simplify paths is to split them when printing. You can do this by selecting the Split Long Paths option and then entering the highest Output Resolution possible (9600 dpi for version 5.0 and later) in the Document Setup dialog box (version 5.0 and later; for version 3.0, see the user guide). At this resolution, the number of split pieces is maximized, creating the least complex file. The program then splits complex paths based on what the printer's memory can handle. The Split Long Paths option does not work, however, on stroked paths or compound paths; to simplify these paths, select the path and split it manually using the scissors tool.

Because the Split Long Paths option can alter artwork, make a copy of your original file before printing or saving with the option selected. Also, be sure to turn off the Split Long Paths option immediately after printing; otherwise, Illustrator will continue to split paths each time a file is saved or printed.

Get to know the filters. Adobe Illustrator 5.0 and later contains numerous plug-in software modules, called filters, that provide shortcuts to previously time-consuming tasks. For example, the Pathfinder filters enable you to create new objects based on the intersections of existing objects in one or two simple steps. Other filters, such as the Artwork View Speedup filter in the Optional Plug-ins folder, accelerate drawing speed. Get to know the contents of your Filters menu and the Plug-ins folders. See the user guide for information on individual filters.

Store frequently used custom colors, swatches, gradients, and patterns. The Adobe Illustrator Start-up file in the Plug-ins folder enables you to customize your Paint Style palette. Each time the program is started, Illustrator loads the information in the startup file. Be sure, however, to keep the startup file clear of unused items, since a large startup file may slow opening of the program.

Working efficiently in Adobe Photoshop

Because Adobe Photoshop files can be very large, the key to optimizing performance in Photoshop is finding ways to decrease the size of your files. Once you've done this and set up your system efficiently, you can avoid many performance problems by working on parts of the file individually or by performing certain tasks on smaller, temporary versions of the file. The Quick Edit module in Photoshop 3.0, for instance, allows you to edit a portion of a file without opening the entire file.

Set your monitor color to 256 or fewer colors. If you don't need precise color previewing in a given work session, set the monitor to 256 colors, gray, or black and white to speed up screen display.

Experiment on a low-resolution version of the file. Often, you can save a lot of time by resampling a copy of the original file to 72 dots per inch and making initial edits and color corrections to the copy. Be sure to save the copy of the file under a different name so that you do not inadvertently replace the original. Once you've figured out exactly which features and dialog box values give you the results you want, open the original file and repeat those steps. If you're adjusting color, save the dialog box settings you use for the low-resolution version and then load them with the original file open. Third-party products, such as Daystar's Photomatic™ and Specular Collage™, let you batch-process image-editing functions.

Use alpha channels and layers. Get in the habit of saving complex selections to channels until you have finished editing a file. This lets you load the selection at any time so that you can easily readjust the area without reselecting. Also, use layers and layer masks to isolate parts of a file and experiment with effects easily and efficiently. If you have many channels or layers, use the Duplicate commands in the palette pop-up menus to copy the channels or layers to another file; then delete them from your working file so they don't increase that file's size.

Make complex selections in Grayscale mode. Because a grayscale image is one-third the size of an RGB image, you can cut processing time by making your selections in Grayscale mode. First, choose Image > Duplicate, and convert the copy to Grayscale mode. Then make your complex selection, save the selection to a new channel, and then load that selection onto the original image. You can boost the contrast of the grayscale image in the Levels or the Curves dialog box to make it easier to select shapes of different colors using the magic wand tool. Alternatively, select the R, G, or B channel that provides the best contrast and make your selections there.

Use Quick Edit mode. If you're editing a portion of a very large file in Photoshop 3.0, you can save the file in Adobe Photoshop 2.0 format, close the file, and then use the Quick Edit Acquire plug-in to open and edit just part of the file. Quick Edit lets you edit a portion of a Photoshop 2.0, Scitex CT, or uncompressed TIFF file without opening the entire file and then save the portion back out to the original file.

Work with two windows open. As with Adobe Illustrator files, you can use the New Window command to avoid having to switch back and forth between views of a file. For example, you can work with two windows set at different magnifications so that you can perform detail adjustments at a high magnification in one window while monitoring the effects on the full-size image in a second window. Or you can make color corrections to an image channel and view the results in both the individual channel and the composite color channel.

Apply filters to channels individually. Some Photoshop filters work in RAM only and do not use the scratch disk. If you're having problems running a filter on a color image, try applying the filter to each color channel of the image individually (with the Wave filter, do not use the Randomize option). Remember that in an RGB image, each channel is one-third the size of the file; in a CMYK image, each channel is one-fourth the size of the file.

Use the shortcuts. As with Adobe Illustrator, you can save a lot of time by learning the shortcuts for tools and commands. These are especially useful for operations that you perform all the time, such as changing magnification or filling selections. For example, double-click the hand tool to fit an image in the window; double-click the zoom tool to display an image at actual size. Press Option+Delete (Macintosh) or Alt+Backspace (Windows) to fill a selection with the foreground color; press Delete/Backspace to fill it with the background color. Get to know the Quick Reference Card included in your Adobe Photoshop package, and put your most commonly used commands in the Commands palette. For *Design Essentials* techniques, load the Design Essentials Commands palette in the Commands Set folder inside the Goodies folder installed with Photoshop.

2 Lines and Perspective

Dashed line effects

Software needed: Adobe Illustrator 3

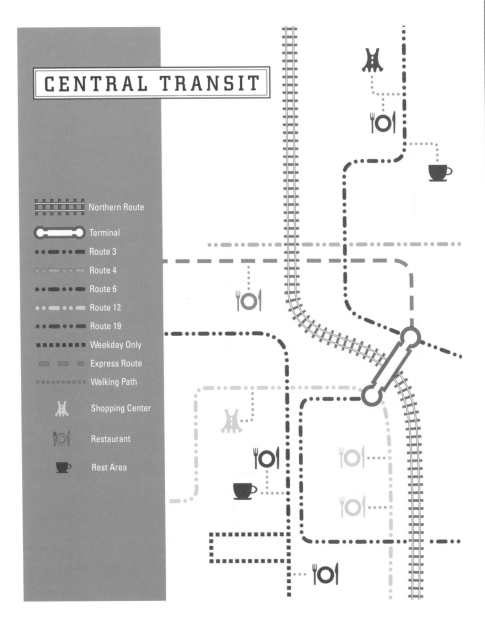

You can generate a variety of useful and decorative effects by varying the dash patterns of your lines and then layering the lines. The following charts provide recipes for just a few examples. To create any of the single-line effects, simply select any line in Adobe Illustrator, open the Paint Style palette (⌘/Ctrl+I), and enter the values shown here. To create the layered-line effects, Option/Alt-select the line (pressing Option or Alt ensures that the entire line is selected), and paint it using the values shown in the first row of the recipe; then copy the line, choose Paste in Front, and paint the copy using the values in the next row of the recipe. Repeat this procedure until all layers have been created and painted. When you have achieved the effect you want, group the lines (⌘/Ctrl+G). Experiment with your own dash patterns to create other effects.

SINGLE LINES	STROKE COLOR	STROKE WIDTH (IN POINTS)	LINE CAP STYLE	DASH PATTERN
	100%	2	ROUND	0, 2
	100%	2	ROUND	0, 4
	100%	2	ROUND	0, 6
	100%	2	ROUND	0, 10
	100%	2	ROUND	20, 16
	100%	2	ROUND	0, 4, 0, 4, 5, 4
	100%	2	ROUND	0, 4, 4, 8, 4, 4
	100%	2	ROUND	8, 4, 0, 4, 8, 10
	100%	2	ROUND	20, 8, 0, 8
	100%	2	ROUND	20, 7, 7, 7
	100%	2	ROUND	5, 6, 5, 10, 15, 10
	100%	2	PROJECTING	0, 5
	100%	2	PROJECTING	0, 10
	100%	2	PROJECTING	15, 5
	100%	2	PROJECTING	15, 7, 0, 7
	100%	2	PROJECTING	20, 7, 7, 7

BUTT   ROUND   PROJECTING

SINGLE LINES

SINGLE LINES	STROKE COLOR	STROKE WIDTH (IN POINTS)	LINE CAP STYLE	DASH PATTERN
	100%	4	BUTT	0.3, 8
	100%	8	BUTT	0.3, 4
	100%	12	BUTT	0.3, 2
	100%	16	BUTT	0.3, 2
	100%	10	BUTT	4, 3
	100%	18	BUTT	3, 4
	100%	12	BUTT	0.3, 2, 0.3, 6, 5, 6
	100%	15	BUTT	2, 4, 10

LAYERED LINES (VALUES SHOWN BY LAYER)

LAYERED LINES (VALUES SHOWN BY LAYER)	STROKE COLOR	STROKE WIDTH (IN POINTS)	LINE CAP STYLE	DASH PATTERN
	100%	5	BUTT	1, 3
	100%	10	BUTT	1, 7
	100%	20	BUTT	1, 15
	100%	25	BUTT	1, 31
	20%	25	BUTT	0.6, 2
	40%	20	BUTT	0.6, 2
	60%	15	BUTT	0.6, 2
	80%	10	BUTT	0.6, 2
	100%	5	BUTT	0.6, 2
	100%	25	BUTT	2, 2
	80%	20	BUTT	2, 2
	60%	15	BUTT	2, 2
	40%	10	BUTT	2, 2
	20%	5	BUTT	2, 2
	100%	20	BUTT	SOLID
	WHITE	15	BUTT	3, 5
	100%	10	BUTT	SOLID
	100%	17.5	BUTT	2.5, 2.5
	WHITE	12.5	BUTT	SOLID
	100%	7.5	BUTT	2.5, 2.5
	WHITE	2.5	BUTT	SOLID

BUTT   ROUND   PROJECTING

LAYERED LINES (VALUES SHOWN BY LAYER)

LAYERED LINES (VALUES SHOWN BY LAYER)	STROKE COLOR	STROKE WIDTH (IN POINTS)	LINE CAP STYLE	DASH PATTERN
	100%	21	BUTT	3, 3
	100%	15	BUTT	SOLID
	WHITE	15	BUTT	3, 3
	WHITE	9	BUTT	SOLID
	100%	9	BUTT	3, 3
	100%	3	BUTT	SOLID
	WHITE	3	BUTT	3, 3
	100%	13.5	BUTT	2.5, 10
	100%	7.5	BUTT	SOLID
	WHITE	7.5	BUTT	2.5, 2.5, 3.5, 0, 4, 0
	100%	2.5	BUTT	SOLID
	WHITE	2.5	BUTT	5, 2.5, 5, 0
	100%	7.5	BUTT	2.5, 7.5
	100%	5	BUTT	5, 5
	100%	2.5	BUTT	7.5, 2.5
	100%	10	ROUND	0, 10
	WHITE	5	ROUND	0, 10
	100%	15	ROUND	0, 15
	WHITE	15	BUTT	1.5, 2.25, 1.5, 9.75
	100%	10	ROUND	0, 10
	WHITE	5	BUTT	5, 5
	100%	12.5	BUTT	SOLID
	WHITE	12.5	ROUND	0, 12.5
	100%	4	ROUND	0, 6.25
	WHITE	4	ROUND	0, 12.5
	100%	1	BUTT	SOLID
	100%	12.5	BUTT	7.5, 2.5, 2.5, 2.5
	WHITE	7.5	BUTT	5, 10
	100%	5	ROUND	0, 15
	100%	12	BUTT	2, 4
	100%	7	BUTT	SOLID
	WHITE	6	BUTT	SOLID
	100%	5	BUTT	SOLID
	WHITE	4	BUTT	SOLID
	100%	4	BUTT	2, 4
	100%	10	PROJECTING	0, 13.5
	WHITE	5	PROJECTING	0, 13.5
	100%	2.5	PROJECTING	0, 13.5
	100%	15	BUTT	15, 2.5
	WHITE	10	BUTT	12.5, 5
	100%	5	BUTT	2.5, 15*
	100%	2.5	BUTT	10, 7.5

*move line down 2.5 points

Shapes with multiple outlines

Software needed: Adobe Illustrator 4 or later, Adobe Type Manager, and Type 1 Fonts

SPECIAL EXHIBITION AT GOLDEN GATE MUSEUM

WOOD

You can create shapes with multiple outlines in Adobe Illustrator by stacking copies of the shapes on top of each other and stroking them with different colors. The last copy of the shape on the stack is filled with a color and no stroke, so that only the outlines of the copies underneath appear around it. This process is analogous to overlaying increasingly smaller pieces of paper—each larger piece of paper creates a frame around the smaller piece on top of it, creating the effect of multiple borders, or outlines.

Before you begin, you'll probably want to determine the best stroke widths for your shape or type outline. Remember that when you stroke a path, Adobe Illustrator creates the border from the center of the path—this means that a stroke value of 6 points will create only a 3-point border outside the path. The stroke value of each consecutive layer determines the width of the border beneath it; for example, a 4-point stroke on top of a 6-point stroke will produce a border of 1 point ($\%_2$ - $\%_2$).

Finally, when stroking type, it's important to copy an unstroked version of the type on top of the stroked type to maintain the integrity of the original letterform.

You can create this type of artwork without using layers, but using layers in Adobe Illustrator 5.0 and later gives you added flexibility. You can then easily edit the artwork on any layer by locking the layers you don't want to modify.

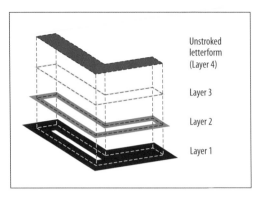

Unstroked letterform (Layer 4)

Layer 3

Layer 2

Layer 1

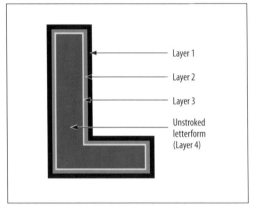

Layer 1

Layer 2

Layer 3

Unstroked letterform (Layer 4)

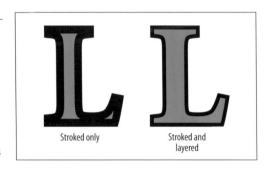

Stroked only

Stroked and layered

1. To create type with multiple outlines, use the type tool to create the word or letters you want to outline, and kern if necessary. Don't kern too much or your letters will overlap after you outline them.

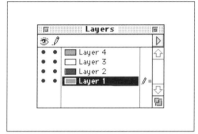

2. If you're using Adobe Illustrator 5.0 or later, choose Window > Show Layers. Create a layer for each colored outline you want on your type or shape. It's helpful to match the selection color of the layer to the color of the stroke you will use. For example, if your stroke will be orange, choose Other as the selection color, and pick a matching orange from the color wheel.

3. With the type selected, open the Paint Style palette (⌘/Ctrl+I). Fill with None, and stroke with the color you want to use for the outermost border. Remember that the stroke width you should use depends on the size of your object and how wide you want each border. In this example, we used a 6-point stroke for the outermost outline of a 72-point letterform.

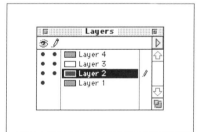

4. Copy the selected artwork (⌘/Ctrl+C). If you're using the Layers palette, lock the bottom layer by clicking the dot in the pencil column next to the layer. Select the next layer by clicking its name.

5. Paste the copied artwork directly on top of the first outline by choosing Paste in Front (⌘/Ctrl+F). If you're using layers, notice that the selected baseline of the type is the selection color you assigned to the layer in step 2.

6. Fill the copy with None, and stroke it with a different color than used for the first layer and a thinner stroke. (We used a 3-point stroke.)

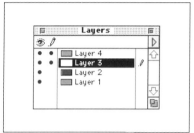

7. Copy the selected artwork (⌘/Ctrl+C). If you're using the Layers palette, lock the active layer by clicking the pencil column next to the layer. Select the next layer.

8. Choose Paste in Front to paste the letters from the Clipboard again; this creates a third layer. Fill this outline with None, and stroke it with a third color and a thinner stroke than used for the second layer. (We used a 1-point stroke.)

9. Repeat steps 7 and 8 until you have as many outline strokes as you want. If you are using type, the final top layer should be filled with a color or white and stroked with None to maintain the integrity of the original letterform.

Variation: If you're using the Layers palette and you want to experiment with different type-faces, simply unlock all layers (click the pencil icon in the Layers palette); then select all layers and choose a different typeface.

Creating offset outlines

Software needed: Adobe Illustrator 5.5

OFFSET AMOUNT: X: 2, 2 Y: 2, 2 **TYPEFACE:** SHINGO MEDIUM **POINT SIZE:** 74 PT	
OFFSET AMOUNT: X: 1, 1 Y: 1, 1 **TYPEFACE:** BAUER BODONI BOLD **POINT SIZE:** 110 PT	
OFFSET AMOUNT: X: 3, 3 Y: 3, 3 **TYPEFACE:** INSIGNIA **POINT SIZE:** 115 PT	
OFFSET AMOUNT: X: 2, 4 Y: 2, 4 **TYPEFACE:** GRAPHITE MM **POINT SIZE:** 108 PT	

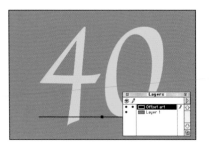

Flat color background

1. Create a background with a solid color. For easy selection in this procedure, open the Layers palette, create a new layer, and name it *offset art*. Create the type or shape you want on this new layer. If you have other layers in your artwork, lock them by clicking in the pencil column next to each layer.

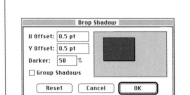

2. Make sure that the offset art layer is selected in the Layers palette and that your artwork is selected. Then choose Filter > Stylize > Drop Shadow. Use the chart at the left to help you decide what offset amounts to use for your typeface size and style. Enter these amounts, make sure that the Group Shadows box is deselected, and click OK.

3. With the shadow still selected, open the Paint Style palette (⌘I). Select the eyedropper tool and double-click the background to fill the shadow with the background color.

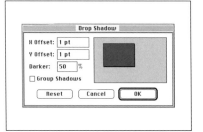

4. With the first shadow still selected, choose Filter > Stylize > Drop Shadow again. Choose a slightly larger amount of offset than you chose in step 2, and click OK.

5. The new shadow is a darker shade of the background color. If desired, change the color of the shadow. Then select all three objects, and group them (⌘G).

Gradient or placed EPS background

1. Create a gradient fill or place an EPS image as the background. For easy selection in this procedure, open the Layers palette, create a new layer, and name it *offset art*. Create the type or shape you want on this new layer. If you have other layers in your artwork, lock them by clicking in the pencil column next to each layer.

2. Make sure that the offset art layer and the artwork is selected. Then choose Filter > Stylize > Drop Shadow. Use the chart at the left to help you decide what offset amounts to use for your typeface size and style. Because you want a bit of the background to show through the offset art, make the offset slightly larger than you would for a solid color background.

3. With the first shadow still selected, choose Filter > Stylize > Drop Shadow. Choose a slightly larger amount of offset than you chose in step 2, and click OK.

4. If you are using type in this procedure, select the three type objects, and choose Type > Create Outlines. If you are using other shapes, continue with step 5.

5. Select the two shadows of the first letter or shape in your artwork.

6. Choose Filter > Pathfinder > Minus Front. This filter subtracts the top shape from the bottom shape. The space that contained the top shadow is now filled with the background image.

7. Repeat step 6 for each pair of shadows in your artwork.

8. Select the letters and their offset outlines, and group them (⌘G).

9. To change the color of the outlines, select them all by first clicking one of the offset shapes with the direct-selection tool and then choosing Filter> Select > Same Fill Color.

10. Use the Paint Style palette to experiment with different colors. Patterns and gradient fills create interesting effects with this technique.

More line effects

Software needed: Adobe Illustrator 5.5

The Layers palette and the new plug-in filters included with Adobe Illustrator 5.5 offer unlimited possibilities for artists to manipulate and customize their artwork. Following are two techniques that take advantage of these features. The first technique shows how to create zigzag and wavy lines using just a couple of standard plug-in filters. The second technique shows how to stack lines with decreasing stroke weights and different colors to get three-dimensional tubelike and neon effects. Using layers to stack the paths lets you easily edit the intermediate paths. Use this second technique in combination with the recipes in "Dashed Line Effects" on page 10 for some interesting effects.

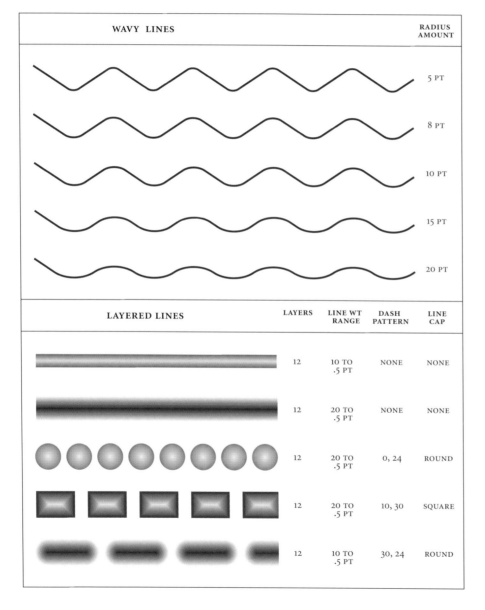

WAVY LINES	RADIUS AMOUNT
	5 PT
	8 PT
	10 PT
	15 PT
	20 PT

LAYERED LINES	LAYERS	LINE WT RANGE	DASH PATTERN	LINE CAP
	12	10 TO .5 PT	NONE	NONE
	12	20 TO .5 PT	NONE	NONE
	12	20 TO .5 PT	0, 24	ROUND
	12	20 TO .5 PT	10, 30	SQUARE
	12	10 TO .5 PT	30, 24	ROUND

Wavy and zigzag lines

1. Draw a horizontal line with the pen tool by clicking to set one endpoint and then Shift-clicking to set the other endpoint.

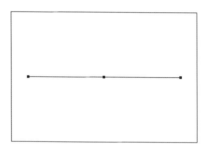

2. To create uniform waves or zigzags, you'll first add evenly spaced points to the line. With the line selected, choose Filter > Objects > Add Anchor Point. This filter places a new point exactly halfway between any two existing points on a selected path.

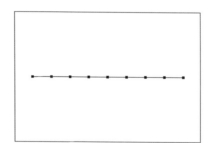

3. Reapply the filter (⌘+Shift+E) until you have a point for each curve in your line.

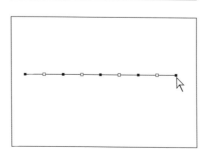

4. Now use the direct-selection tool to select every other point on the line.

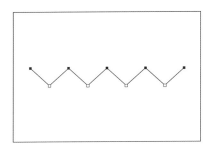

5. Choose Arrange > Move (⌘+Shift+M) or Option-click the selection tool to open the Move dialog box. Enter the height you want for your curves or angles in the Vertical box, and click OK. (You can also use the arrow keys to move the selected points in 1-point increments.) You now have a zigzag line. To make the line wavy, continue with step 6; otherwise, skip to step 7.

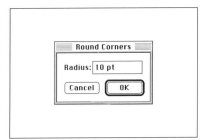

6. With the line still selected, choose Filter > Stylize > Round Corners. Enter the radius you want and then click OK. Refer to the chart at the left to see some waves created using different radius amounts.

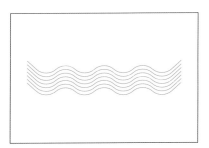

7. To create multiple, evenly spaced wavy or zigzag lines, first hold down the Option and Shift keys to make a copy and constrain its move, and then drag the line up or down. Release the mouse button and then the keys; then choose Arrange > Repeat Transform (⌘D) to make as many evenly spaced copies as you want.

Stacked path blends

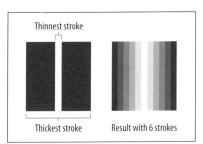

Thinnest stroke
Thickest stroke   Result with 6 strokes

1. First, figure out the total width of your line or tube and the number of gradually thinner strokes you will use to create the 3-D shaded or neon effect. For the best results, the difference in stroke weight between layers should be no more than 2 points. The illustration at the left is a magnification of the strokes used in the following procedure.

2. Open a new file. Create two lines: one with the thickest stroke you will use (the total width of your line) and one with the thinnest stroke. Paint them with the colors you want, and then use the blend tool to create as many steps as you want between the two lines. Each intermediate line represents a layer in your artwork. You will use this blend as a "palette" during this technique.

3. Draw a path that defines the first layer of your line or tube. (If you have many layers in the artwork, you may want to name the layers after the stroke attributes.) Select the eyedropper tool, and double-click the thickest line in the line palette you created in step 2 to copy the line's stroke attributes to the new path.

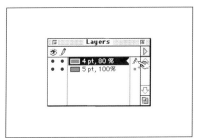

4. Create a new layer. With the stroke still selected, hold down the Option key and drag the colored selection dot from the bottom layer up to the new layer. Release the mouse button and then the Option key. You now have a copy of the line on the new layer precisely on top of the original.

5. Use the eyedropper tool to double-click the next stroke in your line palette and stroke the new line.

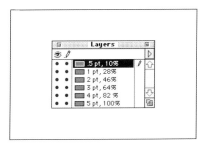

6. Repeat steps 4 and 5 until you have as many layers and stroked lines as you want. Then save the file. You can return to this layered artwork at any time to easily change the color, width, or line attributes of individual strokes.

7. When you are satisfied with the results, copy and paste the artwork into another document. Unless you have turned on Paste Remembers Layers in General Preferences, the artwork will be pasted onto one layer. To keep the artwork perfectly aligned, group it after pasting (⌘G). Grouping also collapses layered artwork onto a single layer.

Creating three-dimensional boxes

Software needed: Adobe Illustrator 4 or later

This technique describes how to use Adobe Illustrator's precision tools to create isometric, axonometric, dimetric, and trimetric views from your two-dimensional artwork. The chart at the end of this technique provides the precise values needed for each type of three-dimensional drawing. If you own Adobe Dimensions 2.0, you can create a three-dimensional box by importing artwork from Adobe Illustrator and mapping it onto a box using the Artwork Mapping feature in Dimensions. To get an isometric view, simply choose Isometric from the View menu. For more information about mapping artwork in Adobe Dimensions, see the Dimensions user guide.

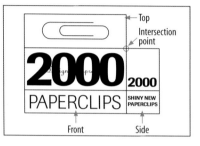

1. Create a flat view of your package, and group each panel (⌘/Ctrl+G). Using the examples shown on the facing page, choose the three panels you need to produce a perspective view, and position them as indicated. The top, front, and side panels will be scaled, sheared, and rotated using the intersection of the three panels as the point of origin.

2. Select the top panel. Then choose the scale tool, and Option/Alt-click the intersection point to set the point of origin and open the Scale dialog box.

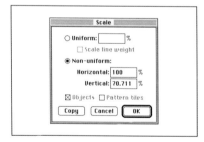

3. Find the vertical scale value for the view you want to create in the chart on the facing page. Click the Non-uniform Scale option, and enter the vertical scale value. (The Horizontal value should be 100%.) In this example, we entered the value for the trimetric 2 view.

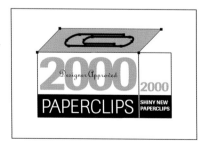

4. With the top panel still selected, choose the shear tool, and Option/Alt-click the intersection point. Shear the panel along the horizontal axis, using the value indicated in the chart.

5. Now you will rotate the top panel so that it appears to recede in space. Choose the rotate tool, and Option/Alt-click the intersection point. Enter the rotate value indicated in the chart, and click OK.

6. Repeat steps 2–5 for the front panel. Be sure to use the numbers indicated for the front panel in the chart. For this technique to work, it's important to follow steps 2–5 in order, first scaling, then shearing, and then rotating the panel, using the intersection point as the point of origin.

7. Repeat steps 2–5 for the side panel, using the next set of numbers in the chart.

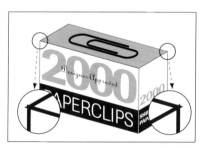

8. If the panel is stroked, zoom in very close on the corner joints to see whether the corners extend past the intersection point, as shown in this illustration. Identify which panels have this problem.

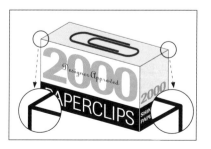

9. To fix the corners, use the direct-selection tool to select the panel edges and then choose the round Join option (the second option) in the Paint Style palette. To enhance the three-dimensional effect of the artwork, paint the panels with slightly different shades and tints. In this example, we lightened the colors on the top panel and darkened the colors on the side panel.

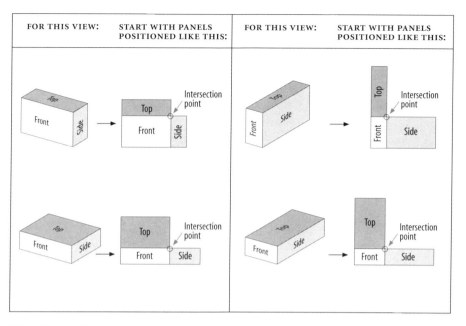

VIEW	A	B	COMMON NAME	FACE	VERTICAL SCALE	HORIZ. SHEAR	ROTATE
				TOP	100.000%	0°	-45°
	45°	45°	AXONOMETRIC	FRONT	70.711%	-45°	-45°
				SIDE	70.711%	45°	45°
				TOP	86.602%	30°	-30°
	30°	30°	ISOMETRIC	FRONT	86.602%	-30°	-30°
				SIDE	86.602%	30°	30°
				TOP	96.592%	15°	-15°
	15°	60°	DIMETRIC	FRONT	96.592%	-15°	-15°
				SIDE	50.000%	60°	60°
				TOP	86.602%	30°	-15°
	15°	45°	TRIMETRIC 1	FRONT	96.592%	-15°	-15°
				SIDE	70.711%	45°	45°
				TOP	70.711%	45°	-15°
	15°	30°	TRIMETRIC 2	FRONT	96.592%	-15°	-15°
				SIDE	86.602%	30°	30°

Creating a three-dimensional pie chart

Software needed: Adobe Illustrator 5.5

The graph tool in Adobe Illustrator lets you create two-dimensional pie charts using data imported from a spreadsheet. Once you are sure that the data will not change, you can add dimension to the graph in Illustrator, or you can bring the artwork into Adobe Dimensions 2.0 to extrude it and render it with shading. If you want to extrude pie pieces by different amounts, Dimensions is especially useful. This technique shows how to add dimension to a pie chart in Adobe Illustrator. For more information about importing Illustrator artwork into Dimensions, see the Dimensions user guide.

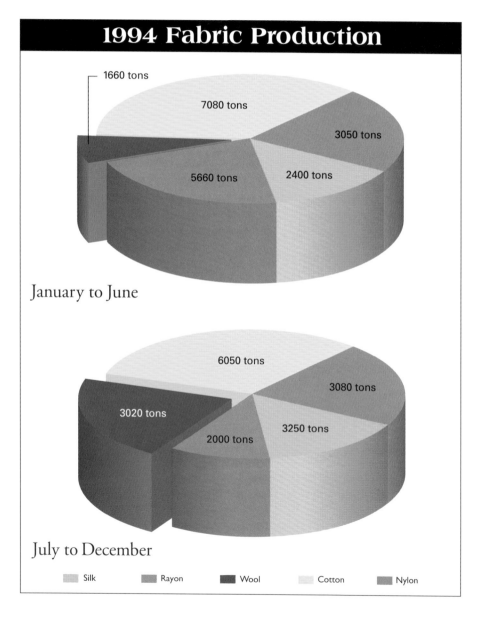

1994 Fabric Production

1660 tons

7080 tons

3050 tons

5660 tons

2400 tons

January to June

6050 tons

3080 tons

3020 tons

3250 tons

2000 tons

July to December

Silk   Rayon   Wool   Cotton   Nylon

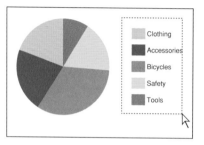

1. Create a pie chart in Adobe Illustrator. Make sure that the Snap to Point option is turned on in the Preferences dialog box (⌘K). Once you are sure that your data is final, make a backup copy of the chart; then remove the graph key and labels using the direct-selection tool to select them.

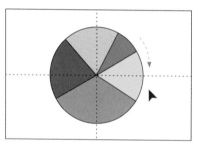

2. For the best results, no side of any pie wedge should be horizontal or vertical. If necessary, select the rotate tool and click the center of the pie; then drag to rotate the pie so that the lines in the pie are angled as much as possible.

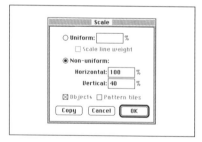

3. First you will add depth to the pie. Select the pie, and double-click the scale tool in the toolbox. Select Non-uniform in the Scale dialog box, and enter a Horizontal value of 100% and a Vertical value of 40%. Click OK.

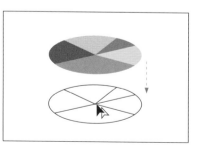

4. To create the bottom of the pie, use the selection tool to begin dragging the pie downward; then hold down the Option and Shift keys to make a copy and constrain its movement. When the copy is directly below the original, release the mouse button and then the Option and Shift keys.

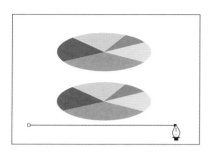

5. Now you will remove the parts of the bottom pie that won't be visible in the final three-dimensional artwork. To do this, you will first slice the pie in half and remove the back half. Use the Shift key and the pen tool to draw a perfectly horizontal line that is longer than the width of the pie.

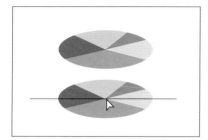

6. Use the selection tool to select a point near the center of the line, and drag the line until it snaps to the bottom pie's center point. The pointer turns white when it is directly on the center point and the status line reads "Snap To."

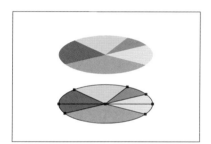

7. Select both the line and the bottom pie, ungroup them (⌘U), and choose Filter > Pathfinder > Divide to slice the pie in half.

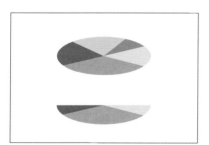

8. Use the direct-selection tool to select the upper half of the sliced pie, and delete it.

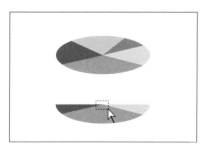

9. Now drag the direct-selection tool to draw a marquee around the center point of the bottom pie pieces. This selects the endpoints of each remaining line in the pie. Delete the points. You will use the remaining part of the pie to build the base and sides of your three-dimensional pie graph.

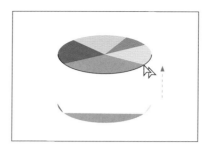

10. With the lower pie parts still selected, position the pointer on one of the points that existed in the lower pie before you sliced it in step 7, and drag the point up to its corresponding point in the upper pie. Hold down the Option key to leave a copy behind. When the double arrows turn white, release the mouse button and then the Option key.

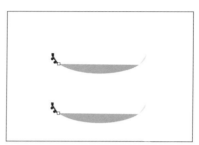

11. You will now create the sides of the three-dimensional pie chart. Select the top pie shape and hide it (⌘3); then select and ungroup the remaining shapes. (The Pathfinder filter regrouped the shapes in step 7.) Use the direct-selection tool to select the leftmost points in the two leftmost curves.

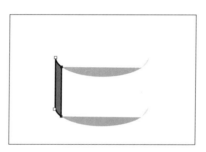

12. Choose Object > Join (⌘J). Then select the rightmost points in the left shape, and choose Object > Join again.

13. Lock the shape (⌘1). Locking will let you easily select the points on the adjacent curves. Repeat steps 11 and 12, working from left to right until all side shapes have been created.

14. Show the top of the pie chart (⌘4), and unlock the side shapes (⌘2). Paint the shapes. For the best results, paint each side shape darker than its corresponding top shape. In this example, we used gradients to fill both the sides and the tops for a shaded look.

Creating a three-dimensional bar chart

Software needed: Adobe Illustrator 4 or later

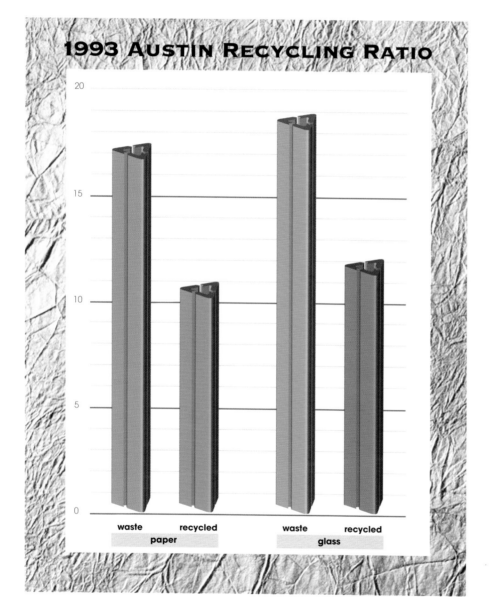

1993 AUSTIN RECYCLING RATIO

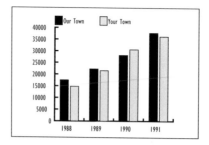

1. Create a grouped or stacked bar chart in Adobe Illustrator. (See the Illustrator user guide for instructions on creating a bar chart.) Make sure that the Snap to Point option is selected in the General Preferences dialog box (⌘/Ctrl+K).

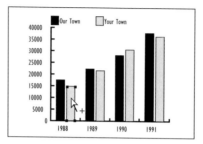

2. Choose the direct-selection tool. Option/Alt-click one of the columns in the graph to select it, and copy it to the Clipboard (⌘/Ctrl+C). Deselect the shape (⌘D).

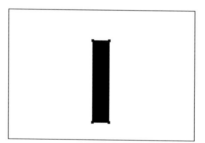

3. Scroll to a blank area of the document and paste the copy of the column from the Clipboard (⌘/Ctrl+V); this will be the bounding rectangle of your three-dimensional graph design. Zoom in so you can draw more accurately.

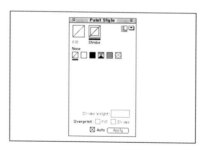

4. Paint the bounding rectangle with a fill and stroke of None; then copy it to the Clipboard.

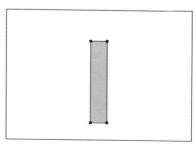

5. To create the face of your three-dimensional graph design, paste another copy of the column directly on top of the bounding rectangle (⌘/Ctrl+F). This ensures that the face of the column aligns with the graph tick marks, and makes the graph easier to read. Paint the rectangle with the color you want to use for the face of your columns (⌘/Ctrl+I).

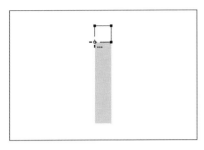

6. With the rectangle still selected, choose the scale tool and Option/Alt-click the upper left corner point of the bar to set the point of origin and open the Scale dialog box. Click Non-uniform, and enter a Horizontal value of 100% and a Vertical value of –20%. Click Copy. (You can change the size of the top by adjusting the vertical scale amount.)

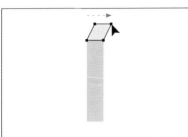

7. Now you will create the illusion of depth. With the top still selected, choose the shear tool and click the lower left corner point. Position the pointer over the upper right corner point, hold down the Shift key, and drag to the right. When you are satisfied with the shear angle of the top, release the mouse button and then the Shift key. Paint the top of the column.

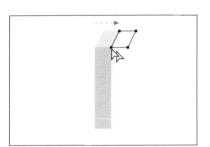

8. Next, create a shape for the side of the bar. With the selection tool, drag the top by the bottom left corner point to the right, holding down the Option/Alt and Shift keys to make a copy and to constrain its movement. When the pointer snaps to the bottom right corner point of the original, release the mouse button and then the keys.

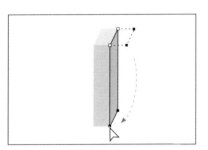

9. Choose the direct-selection tool. Hold down the Shift key and select only the rightmost anchor points of this new shape. Release the Shift key; then drag the shape by its lower right corner point until it snaps to the bottom right corner point of the bar. Paint the side of the column.

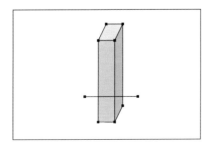

10. Now you will define a "sliding boundary"— a line below which the design will be scaled. This enables the column design to be scaled for different *y*-axis values without distorting the design. Use the pen tool and the Shift key to draw a horizontal line that intersects the column design. Select the entire design, and group it (⌘/Ctrl+G).

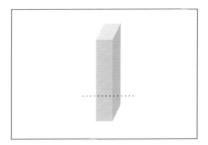

11. Using the direct-selection tool, select the horizontal line and turn it into a guide (⌘/Ctrl+5). (To check that you've done this correctly, use the selection tool—not the direct-selection tool—to drag the column design; the guide should move with the design.)

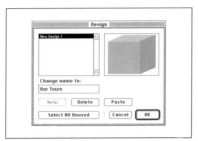

12. With the column design and guide still selected, choose Object > Graphs > Design (Macintosh) or Graph > Define Graph Design (Windows), and click New. Name the design, and click OK. You can now use this design in any column graph you create with the graph tool.

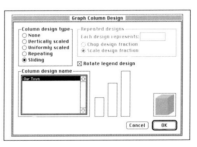

13. Scroll back to the graph and zoom out. Select the graph and choose Object > Graphs > Column (Macintosh) or Graph > Use Column Design (Windows). Click the Sliding option under Column Design Type, select the name of your design, and click OK.

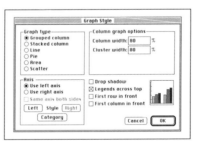

14. To prevent problems in the layering order of the columns, open the Graph Style dialog box, and make sure that the First Column in Front option is not selected. Click OK.

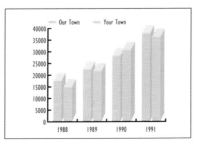

15. Hide the guides. If necessary, use the direct-selection tool to adjust the layering of the axis lines. You can also change the paint attributes of individual columns or column sides. If you want to further embellish this chart in Adobe Photoshop (see page 60), make sure that the segments are not stroked to allow for cleaner selections.

Shaded spherical objects

Software needed: Adobe Photoshop 3.0

You can easily create shaded spherical objects using the gradient fill tool in Adobe Photoshop. This technique shows how to create a shaded sphere and then use the Blur and Offset filters to add dimension to the sphere. Putting the sphere, its shaded area, the highlight, and the background on different layers lets you make changes to the colors at any time without having to remake the sphere. If you want to add a stippling texture to your sphere, create a grayscale sphere and then follow the stippling technique on page 36.

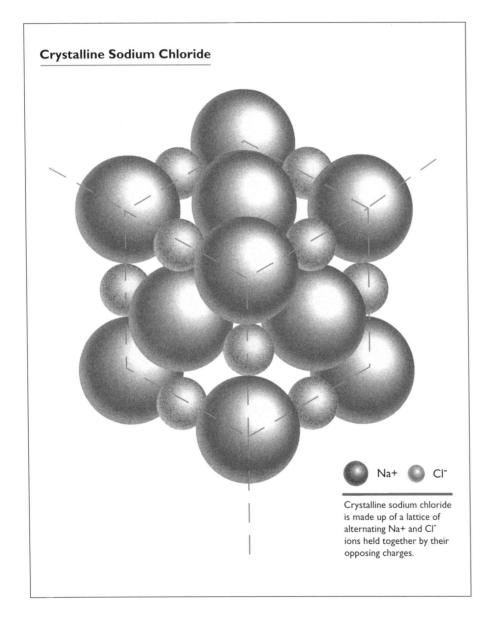

Crystalline Sodium Chloride

Na+ Cl⁻

Crystalline sodium chloride is made up of a lattice of alternating Na+ and Cl⁻ ions held together by their opposing charges.

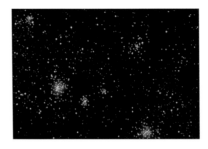

1. Open a new RGB file or the file you want to be the background for the sphere.

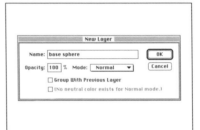

2. Create a new layer, and name it *base sphere*.

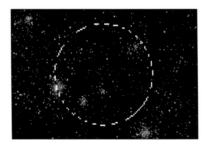

3. Select the elliptical marquee tool by Option/Alt-clicking the rectangular marquee tool in the toolbox or by pressing the M key. Hold down the Shift key and drag to draw a perfect circle. If you want to draw the circle from its center, hold down the Option/Alt key as you drag.

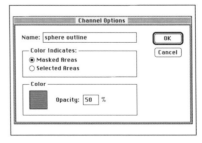

4. Click the selection icon at the bottom of the Channels palette to save the circle selection in a new channel. Then double-click the new channel in the palette, and name the channel *sphere outline*. Reselect the RGB channel.

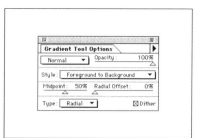

5. Now paint the sphere. Double-click the gradient fill tool in the toolbox, and choose Radial from the Type pop-up menu. Make sure that Foreground to Background is selected in the Style menu.

6. Select a light color or white as the foreground color, and select a medium to dark background color. Position the gradient fill tool inside the selection at the point where you want the highlight on the sphere. Drag to where you want the shadow, and then deselect the sphere (⌘/Ctrl+D).

7. Now you will create a copy of the sphere that you will use to define the shadow area. Click the sphere outline channel in the Channels palette, and choose Duplicate Channel from the palette pop-up menu. Name the new channel *soft offset*. (You can also duplicate a channel by dragging the channel down to the New Channel icon.)

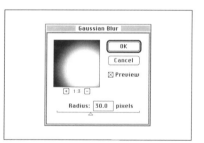

8. Choose Filter > Blur > Gaussian Blur. Select the Preview option, and adjust the Radius until the image is at least as soft as the example shown here. The Radius value you need depends on the resolution of your image and the size of the sphere. Click OK.

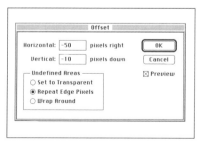

9. Choose Filter > Other > Offset. Click Repeat Edge Pixels, and offset the softened sphere in the direction opposite your radial gradient. For example, if you created your gradient by dragging down and to the right, enter negative horizontal and vertical values. These values determine the size of the shadow area you will define. Note that higher resolution images require larger numbers.

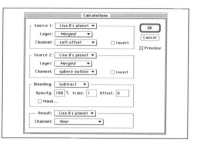

10. To create the shadow shape, you will subtract the offset shape from the outline shape and place the results in a third channel. Choose Image > Calculations. Set up the dialog box so that the Channels and Blending settings are as shown in this example. Click OK. Double-click the new channel in the Channels palette, and name the channel *shadow selection*.

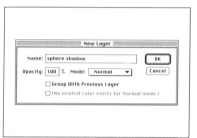

11. Reselect the RGB channel. Then create a new layer, and name it *sphere shadow*.

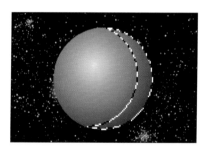

12. With the sphere shadow layer still selected, Option/Alt-click the shadow selection channel in the Channels palette to load the selection.

13. Select a new foreground color for the shadow, and then press Option+Delete (Macintosh) or Alt+Backspace (Windows) to fill the selection.

Enhancement: To emphasize the highlight, create a new layer. Make a small circular selection and fill it with a different highlight color (we used white in this example). Deselect and then blur the highlight using the Gaussian Blur filter. Then use the move tool to position the blurred highlight over the original sphere highlight. If desired, use the Opacity slider to soften the effect.

Perspective grids in Photoshop

Software needed: Adobe Photoshop 3.0

You can create a perspective grid in Adobe Photoshop that helps you match the perspective of imported graphics and images to that of the background image. This technique is especially helpful with images that contain strong perspective lines. To create the grid, you first define the vanishing points in the image; you then use the pen tool to draw grid lines from those points. Once you've created the grid, you distort your imported images or graphics to align with the grid lines. Although you can create a perspective grid either on a layer or in a channel, using a channel requires significantly less memory than a layer.

1. Open the background file.

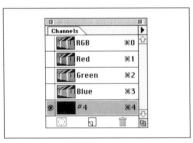

2. To draw the vanishing points for your grid, you will need to temporarily add canvas area to the image. To save the dimensions of the current image, click the New Channel icon in the Channels palette. This creates a channel exactly the size of the current image that you can use later for easy selection. Reselect the RGB channel.

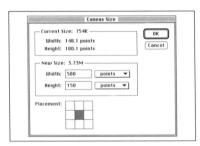

3. Make sure that your background color is white, and then choose Image > Canvas Size. Add enough space around the image to accommodate grid lines that will stretch out past the vanishing points in the image. If the image is oriented horizontally, you will need to increase the width more than the height. If it is oriented vertically, increase the height more than the width.

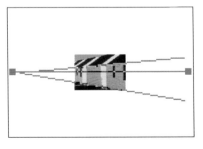

4. Use the pen tool in the Paths palette to draw grid lines that follow the natural perspective lines you see in the photograph. If necessary, use the selection tool to adjust the position of the lines. Once you have created a vanishing point, draw a horizontal line that intersects the point. This line is the horizon line.

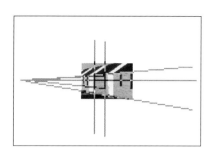

5. Draw any additional perspective lines from the vanishing point that will help you adjust the graphic you want to place in the image. In this example, we drew additional lines as guides for type that we want to place on the building wall. Then save the path by choosing Save Path from the Paths palette pop-up menu.

10. Reselect the RGB channel and then click the eye column next to the grid channel. The grid lines appear on top of the image. Create a new layer for the artwork that you want to add to the image.

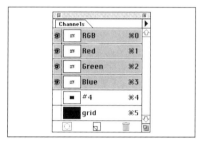

6. You will now add your grid to a new channel. Click the New Channel icon at the bottom of the Channels palette, and name the channel *grid*.

11. Drag or paste the artwork onto the new layer. Align one edge with the positioning guides you created in step 5. If necessary, scale the art-work.

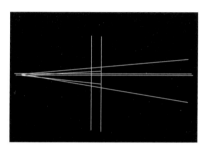

7. Change the foreground color to white, and then select the new path in the Paths palette. Select the pencil tool, and choose Stroke Subpaths from the Paths palette pop-up menu. (You can also press Enter to stroke a path with the selected painting tool.) Deselect the paths.

12. To make the selected object fit to the grid, choose Image > Effects > Distort. Drag each corner of the box to align with your perspective grid lines. When the object is as you want it, click inside the box.

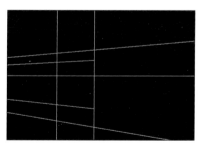

8. Now you will crop the file. Option/Alt-click the channel you created in step 2 to load the channel as a selection. Choose Select > Inverse to invert the selection and then choose Edit > Crop. The file is restored to its original size.

13. Turn off the grid by clicking in the eye icon next to the grid channel in the Channels palette. If necessary, adjust the opacity and the mode of the layer that contains the object. Repeat steps 10-13 for any other objects that you add to the image.

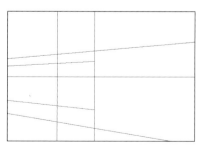

9. Invert the channel (⌘/Ctrl+I) so that when you view it with the image only the grid lines will show.

Perspective grids in Illustrator

Software needed: Adobe Illustrator 4 or later

This technique shows how to use grids in Illustrator to create perspective drawings. To do this, you first set up the perspective grid and create the flat shapes that will appear on the picture plane. Next you draw the sides of the objects along the grid lines and create any receding copies of the elements within the object using the scale tool. The final steps in the technique show how use the blend tool to create repeating horizontal and vertical elements. If you're using Illustrator 5.0 or later, it's a good idea to put different elements of your perspective drawing on different layers. You can then turn layers on and off as you create them to help you focus on each new element in your drawing.

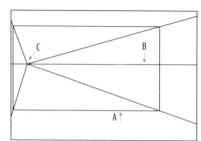

1. Start by drawing a simple 1-point perspective grid. Create a rectangle (A) and a horizon line (B). Then decide where the vanishing point (C) will be. Draw straight lines from the vanishing point past the corners of the rectangle. The lines should intersect the corners of the rectangle.

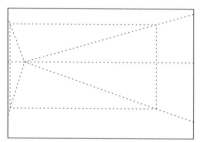

2. Select the lines and the rectangle, and choose Object > Guides > Make (⌘/Ctrl+5).

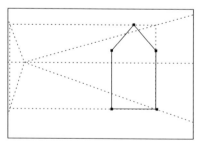

3. Make sure that the Snap to Point option is selected in the Preferences dialog box (⌘/Ctrl+K), and then create the front plane of the first object in your drawing. Draw a flat shape with no distortion.

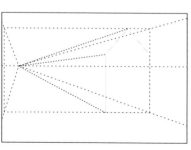

4. Add more guides to help you draw the sides of the shape. Draw the guides from a key point or angle on the shape to the vanishing point. In this example, we added three guides to help us create the side of the building.

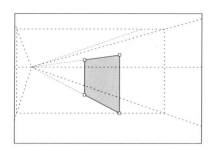

5. Draw the sides of the object using the guides.

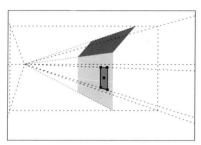

6. Draw any other shapes into the sides of the object, and paint the shapes as desired. In this example, we used the guides to draw a window on the building wall. To create multiple horizontal shapes that recede into the background, first create the frontmost shape and select it.

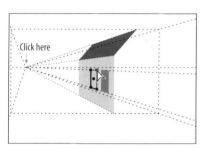

7. Select the scale tool, and click the vanishing point once. Then move the pointer to any point on the selected object that touches a guideline. Begin dragging the point along the guideline toward the vanishing point; then hold down the Option/Alt key to make a copy. Release the mouse button and then the Option/Alt key when the copy is where you want it.

8. To make additional receding copies, choose Arrange > Repeat Transform (⌘/Ctrl+D).

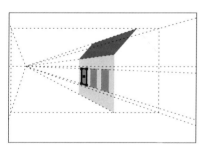

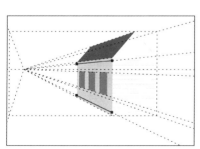

9. To create evenly spaced lines or shapes up and down the sides or across the floor of an object, first draw the two endmost shapes on the side or floor. In this example, we drew lines at the top and bottom of the building sides to create boards. Select both shapes.

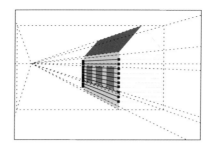

10. Select the blend tool, and click corresponding points of each line or shape. In the Steps text box, enter the number of intermediate shapes you want.

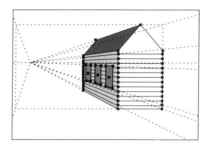

11. If desired, use the scale tool to make additional receding objects. Select all shapes in your object and group them (⌘/Ctrl+G).

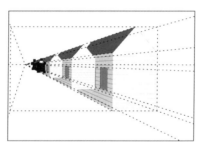

12. Repeat steps 7-8 for each grouped object that you want to duplicate. To get the right effect, you will need to adjust the stacking order of the objects.

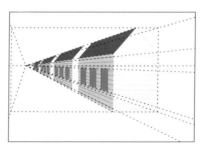

13. Select the second to last shape that you duplicated, and choose Arrange > Bring to Front (Macintosh) or Edit > Bring to Front (Windows). Then select the shape next to it (toward the front of the drawing), and bring it to the front. Repeat this step until you have brought the frontmost object to the front.

14. Create the background objects in the drawing. Make sure that the ground and the sky meet at the horizon line that you created in step 1. If you are using Illustrator 5.0 or later, put the background objects on a new layer to make editing easier.

3 Painting and Blending

Creating impressionist effects

Software needed: Adobe Photoshop 3.0

You can use a variety of techniques to give an image a painterly, impressionistic look. Before layers in Adobe Photoshop 3.0, you had to use the Calculate commands to create these effects. You can still create these effects and more using the Apply Image command; however, for quick and easy experimentation, use layers and layer modes. This procedure describes how to combine a textured image layer with a painted image layer. Using this basic technique, you can apply different layer modes to achieve an almost limitless number of effects. You can also use the Duplicate command to create quick, unsaved copies of an image for experimenting with different features and effects.

TEXTURE RECIPE
NOISE FILTER:
MONOCHROMATIC,
AMOUNT 90

COLOR LAYER MODE
SOFT LIGHT

1. Open the image you want to make impressionistic. Choose Image > Duplicate to make a copy of the file, and close the original. This leaves the original file intact on disk. If the image is a grayscale image, convert it to RGB mode and skip to step 3. If the image is a color image, continue with step 2.

TEXTURE RECIPE
DRY BRUSH FILTER
FROM ADOBE GALLERY
EFFECTS™:
BRUSH SIZE 2,
BRUSH DETAIL 8,
TEXTURE 3

COLOR LAYER MODE
SCREEN

2. Choose Image > Adjust > Desaturate to remove the color from the image.

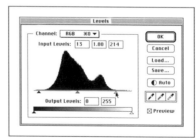

3. Evaluate the image detail. If you need to boost the contrast, open Levels (⌘/Ctrl+L), and move the highlights and shadows input sliders toward the middle of the histogram. Your goal is to retain as much detail in the image as possible.

TEXTURE RECIPE
POSTERIZE:
6 LEVELS

MEDIAN FILTER:
RADIUS 2

COLOR LAYER MODE
COLOR

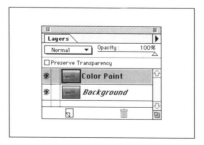

4. Now you will make a copy of the background layer. Drag the *Background* layer in the Layers palette down to the New Layer icon. Then double-click the copy layer and rename the layer *color paint.*

5. Next you will paint in large areas of color on the color paint layer. In this example, we first made a rough selection of the deer with the lasso tool. The selection can be very rough for this effect; it's not necessary to make a perfect mask.

6. Make sure that the color paint layer is the active layer. Fill the selection with a solid color or gradation. Then do the same for other large objects in the image.

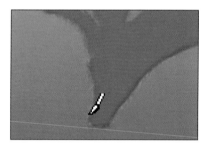

7. Once the large areas have been filled, use the paintbrush to add any small, detailed areas of color. Paint in as much detail as you want in your final image. Try to cover up all of the desaturated, gray areas on the layer.

8. When you have finished painting, click the eye next to the color paint layer in the Layers palette to hide the layer. Then click the *Background* layer to make it the active layer.

9. Now you will create the impressionist texture. Choose Filter > Pixelate > Pointillize. Enter a value between 3 and 5, and click OK. Because the gray in this image is made up of RGB values, breaking the gray into dots creates both colored and gray dots.

10. Now click the eye icon next to the color paint layer in the Layers palette, and click the layer to make it the active layer. Then choose Overlay from the pop-up menu. Overlay blends the color in the top layer while maintaining the texture in the bottom layer. Adjust the opacity if desired, and then save the file.

Enhancement 1: You can use filters to give the pointillized image a finer, grainier texture. Select the background layer in the Layers palette, and choose Filter > Stylize > Diffuse. In this example, we used the Normal setting.

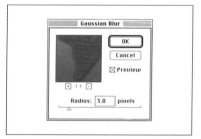

The Diffuse filter roughens the edges of the dots created by the Pointillize filter. Apply the filter again if desired (⌘/Ctrl+F) until the texture is as you want it. In this example, we applied the filter three times.

Enhancement 2: For an even softer look, activate the color paint layer, and choose Filter > Blur > Gaussian Blur. Be sure to select the Preview box to view the effect before applying the filter. If you want to blur by different amounts or just in certain areas, use the blur tool.

To experiment with different colors, make a copy of the color paint layer, and turn off the original. Try using different modes as well. See the chart on the facing page for other examples. When you are satisfied with the results, save the file.

More impressionist effects

Software needed: Adobe Photoshop 2.5 or later

Smudge tool method

1. Open the file you want to alter. Save the file with the filename suffix *.smudged.*

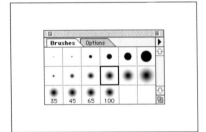

2. Double-click the smudge tool, and press 4 on your keyboard to adjust the pressure to 40%. Then open the Brushes palette and select a medium-sized, soft-edged brush. Keep the palettes on-screen as you may want to change pressure and brush size several times while painting.

3. Begin smudging one of the shapes in the image in the direction of its significant lines, or grain. For example, if you are smudging grass, smudge toward the point of the blades. Change direction for each different shape. For large areas, choose a larger brush. For delicate, detailed areas, use a smaller brush.

4. To correct an area, use the From Saved option of the rubber stamp tool to restore the area, and then try smudging again.

Impressionist tool method

1. Open the file you want to alter. Save the file with the filename suffix *.impress.* It's a good idea to try this technique on a small image first. Because the impressionist tool paints with the last saved version of the file, you won't save the file again until you have finished painting.

2. If you don't want to introduce a new color into your painting by creating a canvas, skip to step 3. To create a canvas for your painting, Select > All (⌘A). Then select a canvas color from the Picker palette or from the artwork using the eyedropper tool (white or black also work well), and press Option+Delete (Macintosh) or Alt+ Backspace (Windows) to fill the image.

3. Double-click the rubber stamp tool, and select the Impressionist option. Select a brush size; in most cases, medium to small brushes give the best results because they allow more detail in the image to show through.

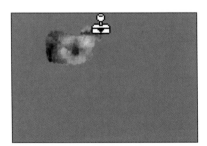

4. Begin painting with the tool. If you created a canvas in step 2, leave some space between your brush strokes for the canvas to show through.

5. Experiment with different brush sizes. To let more of the canvas show through, decrease the pressure of the rubber stamp tool. Save the file only after you have completely finished painting.

Pointillize filter method

1. Open the file you want to alter. Save the file with the filename suffix *.point*. Make sure that the background color in the toolbox is white.

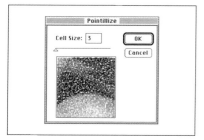

2. Choose Filter > Pixelate > Pointillize. Choose a cell size between 3 and 7, depending on the effect you want. (Note that smaller cell sizes require more memory and take longer to process.)

3. Click OK to create the pointillist effect. The example here was created using a cell size of 3.

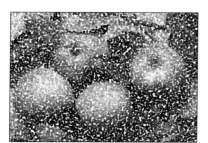

Variation 1: For a coarser texture, use a larger cell size. This example was created using a cell size of 7.

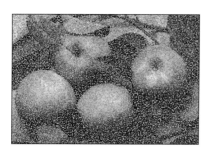

Variation 2: The Pointillize filter fills the spaces between cells with the background color. For a different effect, change the background color. In this example, we used a light orange background sampled from the image and a cell size of 4.

Displace filter method

1. Open the file you want to alter. Save the file with the filename suffix *.displace*.

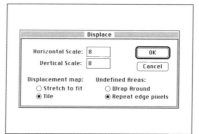

2. Choose Filter > Distort > Displace. Experiment with different Displace filter options to create different effects. In this example, we used Horizontal and Vertical Scale values of 8 pixels and the Tile and Repeat Edge Pixels options.

3. After you click OK, you are prompted to select a displacement map. This is the file that determines how the image is displaced. Predefined displacement maps can be found in the Photoshop Plug-ins folder. The example here was created using the Streaks pattern displacement map.

Variation: You can use any Photoshop file as a displacement map (except bitmaps). This example was created by displacing the magenta, yellow, and black channels using one of the custom textures from page 52 (texture #17). The cyan channel was then offset slightly using the Offset filter.

∾ *Selecting a background color*

To select a background color that goes well with your photograph, try using a color that already exists in the image. To do this, choose the eyedropper tool, hold down the Option key, and drag the eyedropper around the screen. As you do this, the background color displayed in the toolbox changes. Release the mouse button when you have the color you want.

Stippling

Software needed: Adobe Photoshop 3.0, Adobe Illustrator 5.5 or Adobe Dimensions 2.0 (optional)

Use this technique to make shaded shapes appear as though they've been spray-painted with several colors of paint through a stencil. To create this effect, you use the Add Noise filter to create several texture masks and then paint through the textures onto different layers. You do this for each different colored shape in your image. Although the examples here show the effect applied to shaded objects and blends, this technique also works well with flat graphics.

Because the effects of the Add Noise filter vary significantly at different resolutions, in many cases this effect can't be proofed adequately on-screen. You may need to print to accurately proof the results.

1. Create your shaded object in Adobe Illustrator, Adobe Dimensions, or Adobe Photoshop. Make sure that the object is painted with shades of black only. Save the file.

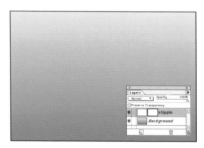

2. In Photoshop, open the background file that you want to use for the stippled graphics. Create a new layer, and name it *stipple.* Then choose Add Layer Mask from the Layers palette pop-up menu.

3. Option/Alt-click the layer mask in the palette to switch your view to the temporary layer mask channel. Then choose File > Place to place the shape you created in step 1. Position and resize the placed object; then click the hammer icon to rasterize the graphics. Do not yet deselect. If you created your shaded object in Photoshop, copy the Photoshop object into the layer mask.

4. Create a new layer, and name it *base color.* (The selection should still be active.)

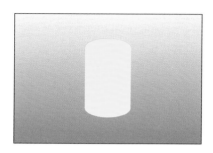

5. Fill the selection with the color you want as the base color behind the stipple colors. Then deselect (⌘/Ctrl+D), and drag this layer in the Layers palette just below the stipple layer.

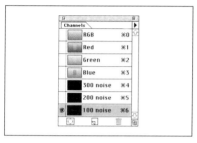

6. Now you will create channels that you will paint through to create the stipple effect. Create a channel for each texture you want in your stippled objects. Name each channel after the amount of noise you will put in that channel. In this example, we made three channels.

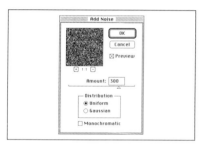

7. To create the texture within the channels, select the first channel you created. Choose Filter > Noise > Add Noise, and apply the amount of noise indicated for that channel in the Channels palette (we used 300).

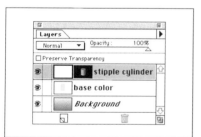

8. Repeat step 7 for each channel you created. Reselect the RGB channel, and click the stipple layer mask. Invert the mask (⌘/Ctrl+I) so that it masks everything but the shape area. Then reselect the layer.

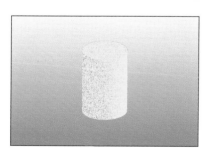

9. Now you will pour the first layer of paint through the first channel. Option/Alt-click the channel with the largest amount of noise to load the channel. Hide the edges so that you can more easily see the results (⌘/Ctrl+H). Select a new foreground color and press Option+Delete (Macintosh) or Alt+Backspace (Windows) to fill the selection.

10. Now add the second layer of texture. Load the channel containing the next largest amount of noise (we used 200). Hide the edges, choose a new foreground color, and fill the selection.

11. Continue loading texture selections and pouring paint through them until you are satisfied with the result. To intensify a color, fill with the same paint twice.

12. When you have finished painting, experiment with other layer modes for different effects. In this example, we used the Hard Light mode to intensify the colors. The effects of the modes vary with different colors.

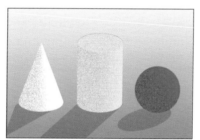

13. Repeat this technique for each different colored shape in your illustration. To save RAM, save a copy of the file, and then merge the layers as you finish stippling each shape.

Cast shadows for objects

Software needed: Adobe Photoshop 3.0

1. Open the image file in which you want a cast shadow. If you plan on separating the final image, convert the images to CMYK mode. This enables you to paint the shadow with a true 100-percent black (K), which helps prevent moiré patterns in the printed artwork.

2. Select the object. (See the selection tip at the end of this procedure.)

3. If the object will be placed on another background, open the background image and use the move tool to drag the selected object onto the background.

4. Double-click *Floating Selection* in the Layers palette, name the new layer *object*, and click OK.

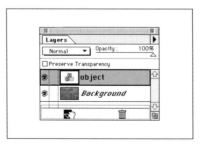

5. Make a copy of this new layer by dragging the object layer in the Layers palette onto the New Layer icon. Double-click the copy layer, and rename the layer *shadow*.

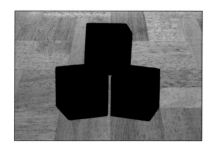

6. With the shadow layer still selected, click the Preserve Transparency option. Make sure that the foreground color is set to 100% black and 0% cyan, magenta, and yellow and then press Option+Delete (Macintosh) or Alt+Backspace (Windows) to fill the object with black.

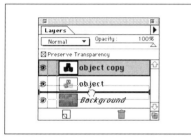

7. In the Layers palette, drag the shadow layer directly below the object layer.

8. With the shadow layer still selected, deselect Preserve Transparency, and choose Image > Effects > Distort. Adjust the shape of the shadow by dragging the endpoints of the selection. Then move the pointer into the selection (the hammer icon appears), and click the mouse button.

9. Now blur the shadow to soften the edges. In this example, we used the Gaussian Blur filter at 10 pixels and then lightened the shadow using the Opacity slider in the Layers palette.

Enhancement: To add a gradation to the shadow, make the shadow layer active, select Preserve Transparency, and choose Multiply from the pop-up menu. Make sure that the foreground and background colors are black and white. Select the gradient fill tool, and drag from the base of the shadow just past the top. Readjust the opacity setting to soften the effect.

❧ *Combining selection tools*

Often the object you want to copy into another file is difficult to select because it contains many different colors and edges. In these situations, you need to rely on more than one selection tool. In the image shown here, the barrel is easy to select because it has smooth edges. The cactus, on the other hand, is difficult to select because its spikes are a different color from both the barrel and the leaves.

To make this selection, we created a selection mask for the cactus and the barrel in stages. First, we used Sampled Colors in Color Range to sample and select the green cactus leaves. We then saved this selection into a new channel by clicking the selection icon in the Channels palette.

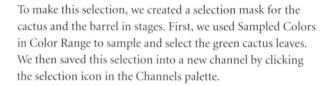

Next we made a rough selection of the cactus plant and used Sampled Colors in Color Range again to sample and select the brownish spikes. The rough selection isolated the cactus so that Color Range would not select brown in any other shapes in the image. Once we had a selection of the cactus spikes, we used Save Selection to add this selection to our existing channel. (You can also add a selection to a channel by Shift-dragging the selection icon in the Channels palette to the channel you're adding to.)

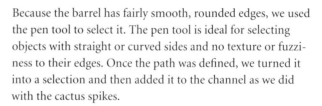

Because the barrel has fairly smooth, rounded edges, we used the pen tool to select it. The pen tool is ideal for selecting objects with straight or curved sides and no texture or fuzziness to their edges. Once the path was defined, we turned it into a selection and then added it to the channel as we did with the cactus spikes.

The final step to creating a selection mask is retouching and cleaning up the mask edges. Sometimes this step can be done in the mask channel. In our example, we loaded the selection onto the image and then used Quick Mask mode to clean up the areas that Color Range missed. We used the paintbrush tool to paint black on areas we wanted to remove from the selection and white on areas we wanted to add to the selection. In the illustration on the right, white is being painted onto spots in the middle of the cactus plant to include them in the selection.

Color-tinted photographs

Software needed: Adobe Photoshop 3.0

In traditional photography, photographers rely on certain post-darkroom techniques to enhance black-and-white prints with color. Sepia toning and iron toning are two of these techniques; these processes tone the overall print with brown and blue, respectively. Hand-coloring with oil paints is another technique traditionally used to add color to photographs—sometimes to make a print look more realistic and sometimes for artistic effect. The following three procedures show how to achieve these traditional photographic effects in Adobe Photoshop.

Color-tinting method 1

1. Open the file you want to color tint. To preserve the original file, choose Image > Duplicate and then close the original. If the file is a grayscale file, convert it to RGB mode. If the file is a color file, choose Image > Adjust > Desaturate to remove the existing color.

2. Because you add color to the image, you must first lighten the entire image so that the color will be visible in shadow areas. Use Curves or Levels to lighten the tones throughout the image. In this example, we used Levels.

3. Select an area or shape that you want to tint. When the selection is as you want it, click the selection icon in the Channels palette. This saves the selection in case you want to make color adjustments later. If you need to limit the number of channels in the file, duplicate the channels into other files using Duplicate Channel in the Channels palette pop-up menu.

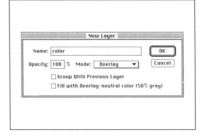

4. Create a new layer, and name it *color*. Choose Overlay as the Mode, and click OK.

5. Now you will begin to add the color tints. Make sure that the selection is still active and that the color layer is still the target layer. Select a foreground color and press Option+Delete (Macintosh) or Alt+Backspace (Windows) to fill the selection.

6. If the color is too intense, adjust the Opacity slider in the Layers palette. Keep in mind that this slider affects everything on a layer. If you want to color tint objects at different opacities, you will have to put each color tint on a different layer and then merge the layers later.

7. Repeat steps 3-6 to complete the image. If your computer has limited RAM and you want to keep the number of layers to two, you can use a single layer for all colors and adjust the opacity using the Fill command instead of the shortcut in step 5. Otherwise, it is faster and easier to create a new layer for each new color tint. Merge the layers when you are satisfied with the results.

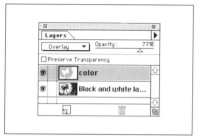

Variation: You can also use a painting tool to paint tints on the color layer instead of filling with color in step 5. Note that you may still want to make selections to protect certain areas from painting.

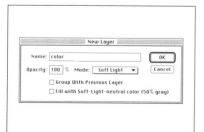

Color-tinting method 2
1. Follow steps 1-5 of color-tinting method 1 but choose Soft Light from the Mode pop-up menu in step 4.

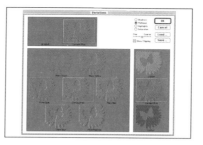

2. Choose Image > Adjust > Variations. Use the Variations dialog box to change the tint of the color. When the effect is as you want it, click OK.

3. Although a color may seem strong in the Variations dialog box, the effect in the composite image using Soft Light mode is quite subtle.

4. If the effect is too subtle, try changing the layer mode to Hard Light and then using the Opacity slider in the Layers palette to tone it down as desired.

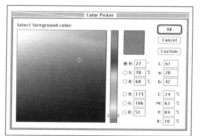

Sepia-toning
1. To make a sepia-tone photograph, follow steps 1-4 of color-tinting method 1. Then make sure that the color layer is active, and choose Select > All (⌘/Ctrl+A). Select a warm brown color as the foreground color.

2. Fill the layer with the foreground color. Adjust the Opacity slider in the Layers palette to increase or decrease the effect. Experiment with different color mixes for warmer or cooler sepia tones. To simulate iron toning, use this technique with a medium blue instead of brown.

Generating smooth gradations

Software needed: Adobe Illustrator 5.5 or Adobe Photoshop 3.0

Shade-stepping, or banding, in printed gradations is caused by a limitation in the number of gray levels an imagesetter can create. The maximum number of gray levels an imagesetter can create is 256. This means that the maximum number of steps that can be used to show a change in color from 0% to 100% of a color is 256. To avoid visible banding in a gradation, each step in the gradation can be no wider than 2.16 points. Whether or not this presents a problem for your artwork depends on the length of the gradation, the colors in the gradation, the tool you use to create the gradation, and—with the Illustrator blend tool—the number of steps you specify. This section explains the factors involved in creating gradations and provides guidelines for avoiding banding in the printed output.

While creating color proofs before going to press is always recommended, it's especially important if your artwork contains gradations. If a project is very critical or expensive, it's a good idea to run a press proof to check for banding and other printing problems. In some cases, banding that appears on film disappears on press. For example, banding in the 0% to 5% area or the 95% to 100% area of a gradation usually disappears on press, because printing presses typically can't hold a dot this small. Banding in the midtone region of a gradation, however, is more likely to appear in the final output.

If you're having banding problems in your printed gradations, you may be able to correct them by taking any of the following actions:

■ Make sure that you're using the best tool to create the gradation (see the following section).

■ Make sure that your resolution and line screen combination produces 256 grays (page 43).

■ Choose the best screening options for your printer (page 43).

■ Increase the percent change in color from the beginning to the end of your gradation (pages 43–44).

■ Decrease the length of the gradation (see page 44–45).

■ If you're using the blend tool in Illustrator, adjust the number of steps in the blend (page 45).

■ Use the Add Noise filter in Adobe Photoshop to mask the banding (page 46).

DESIRED GRADATION	TOOL	METHOD
LINEAR IN ILLUSTRATOR		*To create linear gradations in Illustrator 5.0, use the gradient fill tool. File size (7.5" × 7.5"): 32K.*
DITHERED LINEAR IN PHOTOSHOP		*To create linear gradations in Photoshop 3.0, use the gradient fill tool. File size (7.5" × 7.5"; 300 ppi): 14.5 MB.*
RADIAL IN ILLUSTRATOR		*To create radial gradations in Illustrator 5.0, use the gradient fill tool. File size (7.5" × 7.5"): 32K.*
DITHERED RADIAL IN PHOTOSHOP		*To create radial gradations in Photoshop 3.0 use the gradient fill tool. File size (7.5" × 7.5"; 300 ppi): 14.5MB.*
SHAPE BLEND IN ILLUSTRATOR		*To create shape blends in Illustrator, use the blend tool.*
SHAPE BLEND IN PHOTOSHOP		*To create shape blends in Photoshop, create the blend in Illustrator using the blend tool. Then open the file in Photoshop, and use the Add Noise filter to smooth the blend if necessary.*
LONGER THAN 7.5" IN ILLUSTRATOR		*To create gradations longer than 7.5 inches in Illustrator, create the gradation in Photoshop using the Dither option with the gradient fill tool. Then save the file in EPS format and place it in Illustrator.*
MULTICOLORED IN PHOTOSHOP		*To create multicolored gradations in Photoshop, create the gradation in Illustrator using the gradient fill tool. Then open the file in Photoshop, and use the Add Noise filter to smooth the gradation if necessary.*

Choosing the best tool for your gradation

You can create gradations using the blend tool in Adobe Illustrator, the gradient fill tool in Adobe Illustrator 5.0 or later, or the gradient fill tool in Adobe Photoshop. In general, if you are creating linear or radial gradations, be sure to use one of the gradient fill tools rather than the blend tool.

- Use Illustrator's gradient fill tool for linear and radial gradations that you will print from Illustrator. This tool gives you the most flexibility and the smallest files. In addition, gradations created using the gradient fill tool have fewer banding problems at low resolutions than gradations created using the blend tool.

- Use Illustrator's blend tool for blends between shapes or curved lines. This tool creates larger, more complex files than the gradient fill tool, but is the only tool that lets you create intermediate shapes and curved gradations, such as a gradation that creates shading on the curved surface of a leaf or flower.

- Use Photoshop's gradient fill tool for linear and radial gradients that you will print from Photoshop. This tool works much like the gradient fill tool in Illustrator but includes the Dithering option, which smooths gradations. Because Photoshop's pixel-based artwork is much larger than Illustrator's vector-based graphics, gradations in Photoshop create much larger files than gradations in Illustrator. However, if you plan to bring your Illustrator artwork into Photoshop, consider creating your gradations in Photoshop so that you can take advantage of dithering. For the best printed results, convert the image to CMYK before creating a gradation in Photoshop.

Determining the best resolution/line screen combination

With most printers, increasing the screen frequency decreases the number of gray levels available to the printer. If the number of gray levels is less than the number required for your blend, the result is a posterized gradation. Before you create your artwork, find out what resolution and line screen will be used to print the artwork. If you know the line screen but the resolution hasn't yet been decided, use the table shown here to determine the minimum resolution needed to get 256 levels of gray. For example, if you are creating artwork for a publication that always prints at a line screen of 150, you must print film at a resolution of 2400 or more to get 256 levels of gray. If you print at a lower resolution, you may see banding in your blends. If you can't adjust the line screen or resolution to get 256 grays, find out what these values are, and follow the guidelines described under "Determining the Maximum Length Based on Percent Change in Color," on page 44.

FINAL IMAGESETTER RESOLUTION	MAXIMUM LINE SCREEN TO USE
300	19
400	25
600	38
900	56
1000	63
1270	79
1446	90
1524	95
1693	106
2000	125
2400	150
2540	159
3000	188
3252	203
3600	225
4000	250

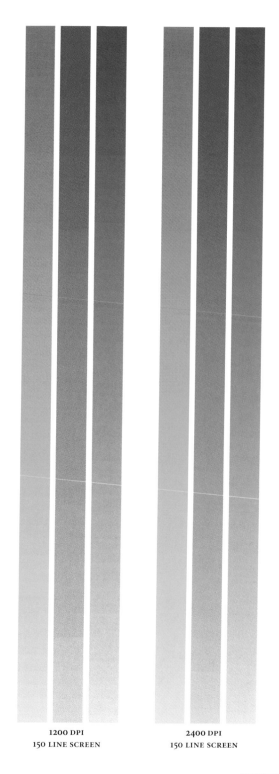

1200 DPI
150 LINE SCREEN

2400 DPI
150 LINE SCREEN

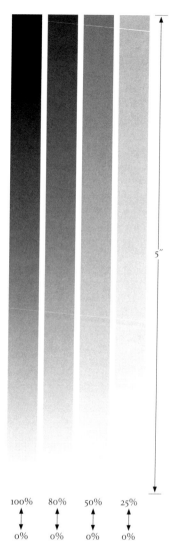

5″

100%   80%   50%   25%

0%   0%   0%   0%

Keep the percent change larger than 50% – These 5″ black gradations were printed at 2540 dpi with a 150 line screen. The two examples on the left contain enough steps to avoid banding; the two on the right do not. Note also that banding is more visible in dark colors than in light colors.

Use the correct combination of resolution and screen frequency – Refer to the table on the left to find the correct resolution to use with your line screen. The three blends shown on the left contain banding caused by the wrong resolution/line screen combination.

Choosing screening options

In both Adobe Photoshop and Adobe Illustrator, the Use Printer's Default Screens option is selected by default for all new files. In Photoshop, you can deselect this option and specify your own screens. To open the Halftone Screens dialog box, choose File > Page Setup and click Screens.

Adobe Illustrator uses the printer's default screens for all printing over 600 dpi, regardless of whether the Use Printer's Default Screens option is selected or not. If you create gradations in Illustrator using the gradient fill tool, however, Illustrator turns off the Use Printer's Default Screens option for that file and uses its own screens for low-resolution printing. In most cases, Illustrator's screens ensure smoother gradients at low resolutions. You may, however, want to turn the option on if your printer includes a special screening technology, such as stochastic screening.

If you're unsure whether to use the printer's screens at low resolution, try printing the artwork both with and without the option selected. In Illustrator, the Use Printer's Default Screens option is located in the Document Setup dialog box.

Finally, if you have trouble printing gradient fills from Illustrator and you are using an older imagesetter or laser printer, try turning on the Compatible Gradient Printing option in the Document Setup dialog box. Be sure to turn this option on only with files that contain gradient fills and only when printing to an older printer, however, because it will slow printing in other situations.

Determining the maximum length based on percent change in color

To avoid banding in printed gradations, it's important to make sure that each step, or *band,* in the gradation does not exceed a width of 2.16 points. The width of the gradation bands is determined by two factors: the number of steps, or gray levels, in the gradation and the length of the gradation.

The number of steps in a gradation is determined by the percent change in color from the beginning to the end of the gradation. With blends between process color mixes, the number of steps is determined by the largest percent change in any of the color components. For example, a gradation from 10% yellow and 50% magenta to 80% yellow and 70% magenta indicates a 70% change, dictated by the change in yellow.

The chart on the facing page shows the maximum gradation lengths for different percent changes in color printed on an imagesetter that is producing 256 gray levels. To figure out the maximum length for other percent changes, or if your line screen/resolution combination is not giving you 256 gray levels (see page 43), use the following formula:

Maximum blend length = 2.16 points × Number of grays × Percent change in color

Determining the maximum blend length for Illustrator's blend tool

Adobe Illustrator's blend tool calculates the number of steps required for each blend based on the percent change in color in the blend. You can use this number to quickly determine whether your blend is too long for the number of steps required. Note that Illustrator's recommended number of steps are based on the assumption that the blend will be printed with a line screen and resolution combination that provides 256 levels of gray. If this is not the case, or if you are using a tool other than the blend tool, see the previous section, "Determining the Maximum Length Based on Percent Change in Color."

1. Create the beginning and ending shapes of your blend. Select the measure tool, and click the top leftmost point of the two lines or shapes; then click the corresponding point of the right line or shape.

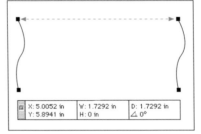

2. Write down the distance displayed in the Info window. This distance represents the length of your blend and is displayed in inches, points, or centimeters, depending on the ruler units specified in the Preferences dialog box. Click OK.

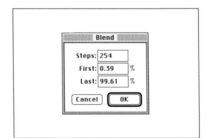

3. Make sure that both shapes are selected, click the blend tool, and then click corresponding points of the two shapes. The number of steps required for the blend appears in the Blend dialog box. Look at the table on page 45 to find out if the length that you wrote down in step 2 is greater than the maximum length indicated in the chart.

4. If the length is within the range indicated, click OK to create the blend. If it isn't, reduce the length of the blend, increase the percent change in color, or use the Add Noise filter to smooth the blend (see page 46). Remember that the percent change in color is determined by the largest percent change in the components of a process color mix.

PERCENT CHANGE	NUMBER OF STEPS ADOBE ILLUSTRATOR RECOMMENDS	MAXIMUM BLEND LENGTH		
		POINTS	INCHES	CMS
0	10	21.6	.3	.762
0	20	43.2	.6	1.524
0	30	64.8	.9	2.286
0	40	86.4	1.2	3.048
0	50	108.0	1.5	3.810
0	60	129.6	1.8	4.572
0	70	151.2	2.1	5.334
0	80	172.8	2.4	6.096
0	90	194.4	2.7	6.858
0	100	216.0	3.0	7.620
0	110	237.6	3.3	8.382
0	120	259.2	3.6	9.144
0	130	280.8	3.9	9.906
0	140	302.4	4.2	10.668
0	150	324.0	4.5	11.430
0	160	345.6	4.8	12.192
0	170	367.2	5.1	12.954
0	180	388.8	5.4	13.716
0	190	410.4	5.7	14.478
0	200	432.0	6.0	15.240
0	210	453.6	6.3	16.002
0	220	475.2	6.6	16.764
0	230	496.8	6.9	17.526
0	240	518.4	7.2	18.288
0	250	540.0	7.5	19.050
0	256	553.0	7.7	19.507

The percent change in color determines the maximum length a gradation can be without banding. Because each step width in a gradation should not exceed 2.16 points, you can predict banding in a gradation based on the number of steps in the gradation and the gradation length. This chart shows maximum gradation lengths for different percent changes in color printed using a line screen and resolution combination that produces 256 gray levels. The second column in this chart shows the number of steps recommended by Illustrator's blend tool for each percent change in color; this number indicates the number of gray levels that can be used to print the blend.

Using formulas to determine the number of steps with the blend tool

If you've found that the resolution and line screen combination you are using to print your artwork does not give you 256 grays, you still might be able to avoid banding in gradations created using the blend tool by changing the number of steps in the Blend dialog box. To do this, use the following procedure:

1. Calculate the number of grays available for your output using the following formula:

Number of grays = {Resolution (dpi) = Line screen (lpi)}^{2}

2. Calculate the number of steps available for your blend using the following formula:

Number of steps = Number of grays ÷ Percent change in color

To figure out the percent change in color, subtract the lower value from the higher value (for example, a blend between 50% black and 100% black indicates a 50% change in color.) When blending process color combinations, identify the largest percent change between process colors.

3. Enter the number of steps from step 2 in the Blend dialog box. Entering fewer steps than this will give you fewer gray levels than are available, and so may cause banding; entering more steps will increase the file size with no improvement in the printed output.

4. Now calculate the width of each step in the gradation. If the step width is 2.16 points (.03 inches) or less, you should not get banding in the final output. If the width is greater than 2.16 points, you may get banding, depending on the colors in the gradation. If you get banding, decrease the length of the gradation, increase the percent change in color, or use the Add Noise filter in Adobe Photoshop to smooth the gradation as described in the following section.

Step width = Blend length ÷ Steps available

Adding noise to smooth out gradation banding

You can also use the Adobe Photoshop Add Noise filter to compensate for banding in gradations created in Illustrator. The Add Noise filter compensates for banding in two ways. First, it tricks the eye into seeing more shades of gray than the printer can produce by randomly scattering the available shades into a pattern, creating a dithering effect. Second, the Add Noise filter covers up flaws and streaks by adding pixels. To ensure that the filter doesn't create new color values in the image, it's important to apply the filter to each channel individually.

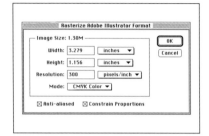

1. Open the file containing the gradation. Make a selection around the gradation to protect the rest of your image.

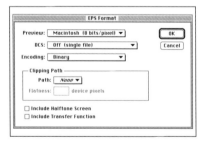

2. Select each of the individual color channels (Cyan, Magenta, Yellow, and Black), and apply the Add Noise filter to each channel that displays the gradation image. Do not apply the filter to a channel if it contains no visible image. Refer to the sample blends on the right to determine the amount of noise needed for your blend.

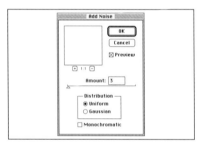

3. To use this file in other documents, choose File > Save a Copy. The Save a Copy dialog box lets you save a flattened file version of the file in any format without affecting your current file.

Use these examples to help you determine the amount of noise needed to smooth out your blend. Notice that in the examples created using large amounts of noise, the white areas of the blends take on a subtle tone of color.

0 3 5 7 10
AMOUNT OF NOISE ADDED

4 Patterns and Textures

Constructing simple patterns

Software needed: Adobe Illustrator 4 or later

The simplest way to construct a pattern tile is to draw any graphic object and surround it with a rectangle placed in the background. This procedure describes how to create dense patterns that tile perfectly by positioning copies of the desired graphic in each corner of the pattern rectangle. Once you've created the pattern, you can use it in your artwork and embed it in other documents; you can then alter the pattern in the artwork without changing the original design.

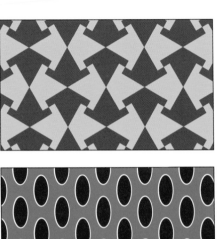

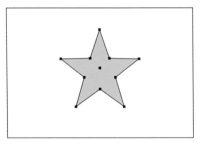
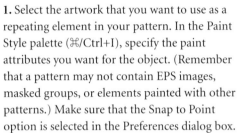

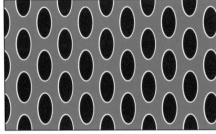
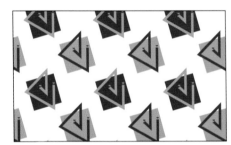
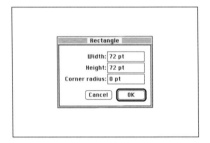

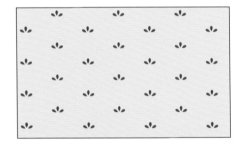

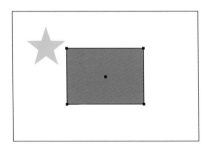

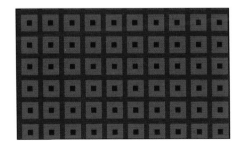
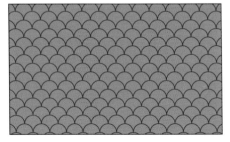
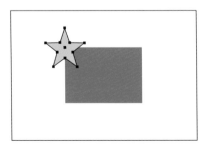

1. Select the artwork that you want to use as a repeating element in your pattern. In the Paint Style palette (⌘/Ctrl+I), specify the paint attributes you want for the object. (Remember that a pattern may not contain EPS images, masked groups, or elements painted with other patterns.) Make sure that the Snap to Point option is selected in the Preferences dialog box.

2. Draw a rectangle the size you want the pattern tile. For the fastest tiling and printing, the rectangle should be about one square inch. If necessary, you can start with a larger rectangle and then scale it down in step 9. Note that the rectangle must have square corners—that is, if you use the rectangle tool, the corner radius must be 0.

3. The paint attributes of the rectangle define the pattern's background. Fill and stroke the rectangle with None for a transparent background, or paint it for a solid background. If you want the tile boundaries to be outlined in the final pattern, stroke the rectangle. Then send the rectangle to the back (⌘- on the Macintosh; Ctrl+Shift+B with Windows).

4. Position the object over the left corner of the rectangle.

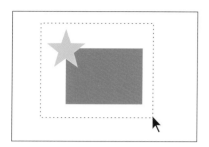

5. Select both the rectangle and the object.

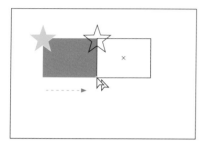

6. Position the pointer on the lower left corner of the rectangle, and begin dragging the artwork to the right; then hold down the Option/Alt and Shift keys to create a copy and to constrain its movement horizontally. When the left corner of the new rectangle snaps to the right corner of the original, release the mouse button and then the keys.

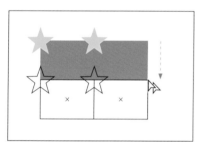

7. Select all of the pattern artwork. Begin dragging the artwork downward by one of the upper corner points; then hold down the Option/Alt and Shift keys to create a copy and to constrain its movement. When the upper corner of the copy snaps to the lower corner of the original, release the mouse button and then the keys.

8. Delete all rectangles but the first (in this case, the upper left rectangle). The remaining rectangle defines the boundaries of the pattern tile.

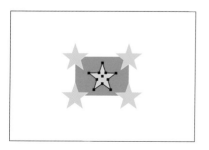

9. Place any additional graphics you want within the rectangle. Make sure that these elements don't overlap the bounding rectangle; if they do, the pattern won't tile correctly. If you began with a rectangle larger than one square inch, scale the artwork now for more efficient tiling.

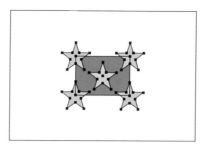

10. Select the rectangle and its contents.

11. Choose Object > Pattern (Macintosh) or Paint > Pattern (Windows), and click New. A preview of the new pattern tile appears in the upper right corner of the dialog box. Name the pattern, and click OK; the new pattern is now embedded in your artwork.

12. Create a shape, and use the Paint Style palette to fill it with your new pattern.

Using patterns to create textures

Software needed: Adobe Illustrator 4 or later

You can create the effect of an uneven texture by constructing a pattern that appears irregular when it tiles. To achieve this effect, the edges of the pattern tile must match up perfectly so that the tiling results in one continuous texture.

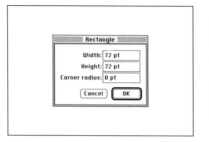

1. Make sure that the Snap to Point option is turned on in the Preferences dialog box (⌘K). Use the rectangle tool to draw the bounding rectangle for your pattern tile. For efficient printing, the finished tile should be approximately one square inch; if you wish, you can start with a larger rectangle and scale it in step 10.

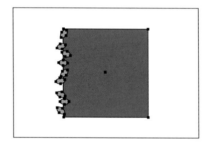

2. Fill the rectangle with the background you want for your pattern tile (fill it with None for a transparent background). Begin drawing your texture with shapes or lines that intersect only the left side of the rectangle. When you have finished, select the rectangle and the texture.

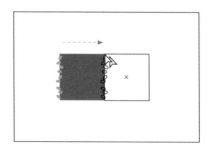

3. Position the pointer on the upper left corner of the rectangle. Begin dragging the artwork to the right; then press the Option/Alt and Shift keys to make a copy and to constrain its movement horizontally. When the upper left corner of the copy snaps to the upper right corner of the original, release the mouse button and then the keys.

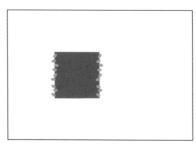

4. Select the right rectangle and delete it.

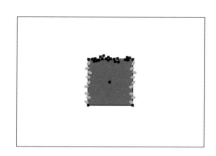

5. Continue drawing your texture with shapes or lines that intersect only the top of the rectangle. When you have finished, select the rectangle and the top texture.

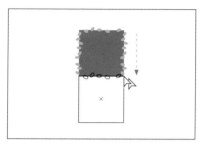

6. Position the pointer on one of the upper corner points of the rectangle. Begin dragging the selected artwork downward; then press the Option/Alt and Shift keys to make a copy and constrain its movement. When the upper corner of the copy snaps to the lower corner of the original, release the mouse button and then the keys.

7. Select the lower rectangle, and delete it.

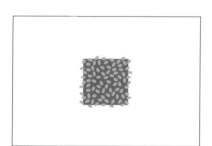

8. Fill in the middle of the rectangle with your texture. Be careful not to intersect any of the rectangle's edges or corners.

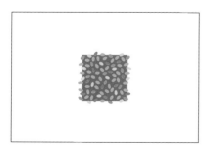

9. For a more varied texture, try using more than one color for the texture elements. Remember that contrasting colors may stand out and create a recognizable pattern. Subtle color differences, however, may enhance the illusion that this is a texture and not a repeating pattern.

10. Select the pattern tile. If you began with a rectangle larger than one square inch, scale the artwork for more efficient tiling. With the tile still selected, choose Object > Pattern (Macintosh) or Paint > Pattern (Windows), and click New. A preview of the pattern tile appears in the upper right corner of the dialog box. Name the new pattern, and click OK.

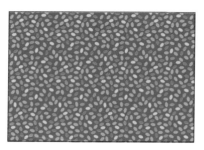

11. You are now ready to test the pattern tile. Create a shape, open the Paint Style palette (⌘/Ctrl+I), and fill the shape with your new pattern.

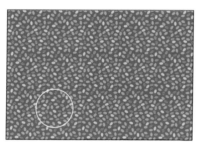

12. Now use the zoom tool to reduce your view of the artwork, and look for places in the texture that create an obvious repeating pattern. If possible, print the pattern tile and mark the areas that need work.

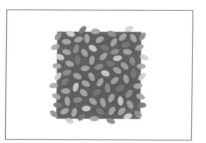

13. Return to the pattern tile, and adjust the artwork to correct the problem areas. Note that if you adjust any artwork that intersects a tile edge, you will need to repeat steps 3 and 4 or steps 6 and 7. Continue adjusting your pattern tile and previewing the textured area until no repeating patterns are obvious.

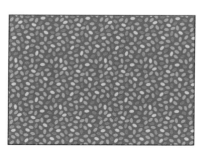

14. When you are satisfied with the tile, redefine the pattern in the Pattern dialog box, and click OK. Then fill your shape with the new pattern.

Custom textures

Software needed: Adobe Photoshop 3.0

To add texture to an Adobe Photoshop image, you can define a texture as a pattern and paint with it, or you can add texture to a layer mask between two layers. Most of the color samples shown here were created by filling the background layer with a color, filling a second layer with another color, and then applying filters to a layer mask to create the texture.

All of these examples were created at an image resolution of 200 pixels per inch; different image resolutions will produce different results. At lower resolutions, the textures appear coarser; at higher resolutions, they are more subtle. If you're working with different resolutions, be sure to proof the results on the output device you will use for the final printed piece.

MASK LAYER   **RESULT**

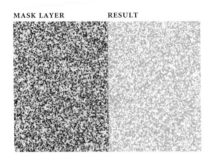

Texture 1:
Pointillize filter: Cell Size 3
Adjust Levels (⌘/Ctrl+L) until input reads
   212, 0.26, 255
Add Noise filter: 32, Gaussian
Equalize (⌘/Ctrl+E)
Add Noise filter: 32, Gaussian

Texture 2:
Add Noise filter: 300, Gaussian

Texture 3:
Add Noise filter three times: 300, Gaussian

Texture 4:
Add Noise filter three times: 300, Gaussian
Displace filter: 10 Horizontal and Vertical Scale,
   Stretch to Fit, Wrap Around, Random Strokes

MASK LAYER   **RESULT**

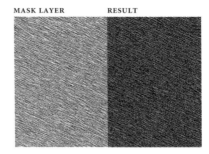

Texture 5:
Add Noise filter three times: 300, Gaussian
Motion Blur filter: 21° Angle, 10 Pixel Distance
Sharpen filter four times

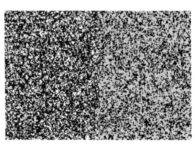

Texture 6:
Add Noise filter: 300, Uniform
Ripple filter: 200, Small
Posterize: 2 Levels
Diffuse: Darken Only

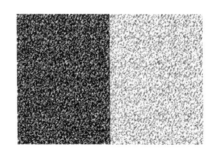

Texture 7:
Open Intricate Surface pattern: 72 ppi (Patterns
   folder)
Select All (⌘/Ctrl+A) and Define Pattern
Fill layer mask with 100% Pattern
Diffuse filter: Normal
Invert (⌘/Ctrl+I)

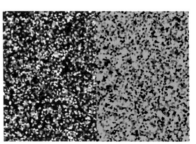

Texture 8:
Add Noise filter: 300, Uniform
Crystallize: Cell Size 5

Texture 9:
Fill layer mask with 50% Black
Add Noise filter: 5, Gaussian
Adjust Levels (⌘/Ctrl+L): click Auto button
Wind filter three times: Stagger, Right

Texture 10:
Fill layer mask with 50% Gray
Pointillize filter: Cell size 5
Adjust Levels (⌘/Ctrl+L): click Auto button
Motion Blur filter: -45° Angle, 2 Pixel Distance
Unsharp mask filter: 200%, Radius 5, Threshold 3

Texture 11:
Add Noise filter: 300, Gaussian
Motion blur filter: -37° Angle, 20 Pixel Distance
Unsharp mask filter: 163%, Radius 4.5,
   Threshold 15

Texture 12:
Fill layer mask with 25% Black
Add Noise filter: 100, Gaussian
Emboss filter: 30° Angle, 3 Height, 100%

Texture 13:
Fill layer mask with 25% Black
Add Noise filter: 100, Gaussian
Emboss filter: 30° Angle, 3 Height, 100%
Motion Blur filter: 30° Angle, 10 Pixel Distance

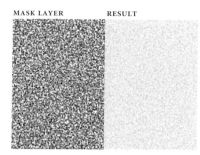

Texture 14:
Fill layer mask with 100% Black
Add Noise filter: 50, Uniform
Pointillize filter twice: Cell Size 3

Texture 15:
Open Random V's: 72 ppi (Patterns folder)
Select All (⌘/Ctrl+A) and Define Pattern
Fill layer mask in texture file with 100% pattern
Ripple filter: 200, Small

Texture 16:
Open Herringbone 2: 72 ppi (Patterns folder)
Select All (⌘/Ctrl+A) and Define Pattern
Fill layer mask in texture file with 100% Pattern
Diffuse filter three times: Lighten Only
Add Noise filter: 100, Gaussian

Texture 17:
Fill layer mask with 50% Gray
Pointillize filter: Cell size 6
Ripple filter: 200, Large

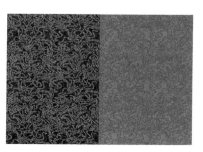

Texture 18:
Open Wrinkle: 100 ppi (Patterns folder)
Select All (⌘/Ctrl+A) and Define Pattern
Fill layer mask in texture file with 50% Pattern
Invert (⌘/Ctrl+I)
Diffuse Filter: Lighten Only
Sharpen filter
Add Noise filter: 50, Uniform

Making a seamless pattern

Software needed: Adobe Photoshop 2.5 or later

To make a pattern in Adobe Photoshop, you simply select an area using the rectangular selection tool and then choose Edit > Define Pattern. Almost always, however, filling an area with this pattern will leave telltale tiling lines, or grids. For a pattern to tile seamlessly, the edges of the pattern tiles must align exactly to create a continuous image. This technique shows how to create a pattern tile whose edges won't be visible when the tile repeats.

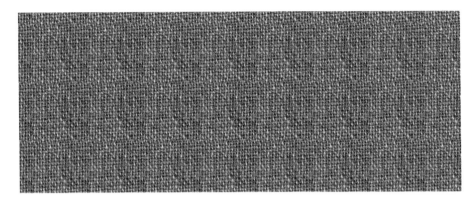

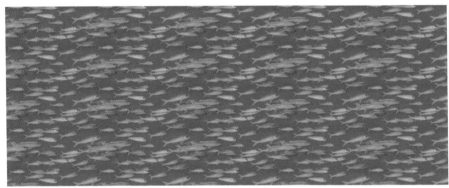

1. Open the image that contains the area you want to make into a pattern tile.

2. Crop the image to the size and area you want the pattern tile to be.

3. Check the size of the file by holding down Option/Alt and selecting the size box in the lower left corner of the window. Divide the pixel width and height by two and make a note of the resulting values for the next step. (If the width or height is an odd number, round it up before dividing.)

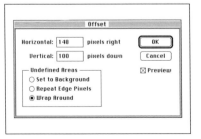

4. Choose Filter > Other > Offset. Select the Wrap Around option, and enter the values you calculated in step 3. The Horizontal value should be half the pixel width of the file; the Vertical value should be half the pixel height.

5. Click OK. The Offset filter splits the image into four sections. Notice that the left half of the image completes the right half and the top half of the image completes the bottom half.

6. Now use the rubber stamp tool to remove the center seam between the four sections of the image. Double-click the rubber stamp tool, select the Clone (aligned) option, and decrease the opacity to less than 100%. (We used 50%.) Select a soft brush from the Brushes palette.

7. Option/Alt-click to sample an image or texture area that you want to clone over the seam.

8. Begin cloning using multiple, short brush strokes so that the stroke itself is not visible. Continue sampling until you have covered the seam. In this example, we cloned several different flowers and flower parts over the seam.

9. Next you will test the pattern tile for any holes in the tile that will create recognizable tiling. Choose Select > All (⌘/Ctrl+A); then choose Edit > Define Pattern.

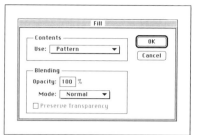

10. Create a new file to use as a pattern fill test. Make sure that the file is several times larger than the pattern tile. Select a large area (or the entire file), and choose Edit > Fill. From the Use pop-up menu, choose Pattern. Use a mode of Normal and an opacity of 100% so that you can easily identify any holes in the pattern. Click OK.

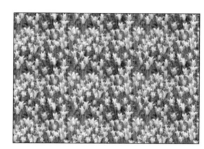

11. Evaluate the overall look of the pattern and identify the problem areas. If you like the effect, save the pattern tile file. If you want to touch up the tile, continue with step 12.

12. To further even out the overall texture of the pattern, return to the pattern tile file and clone more of the image in areas that appear bare in the test file. Keep the pattern test file visible so that you can refer to it as you touch up the tile.

13. Choose Select > All (⌘/Ctrl+A) and then Edit > Define Pattern to redefine the pattern. Return to the pattern test file, and fill the file or selection with the newly defined pattern. Evaluate the overall effect and correct the tile again if necessary.

Using Illustrator pattern tiles in Photoshop

Software needed: Adobe Illustrator 5.5, Adobe Photoshop 3.0, Adobe Collectors Edition Patterns and Textures (optional)

Adobe Collectors Edition: Patterns and Textures is a set of predesigned patterns for use with Adobe Illustrator. A small number of pattern tiles from this set are included with the Adobe Photoshop program. This technique describes how to use other patterns from the Collectors Edition set—as well as custom patterns you create in Illustrator—in Adobe Photoshop. Note that for the best results, you should use this technique only with Illustrator 5.5. Earlier versions of Illustrator may round up the dimensions of the pattern tile and so create gaps in the pattern when it tiles in Photoshop.

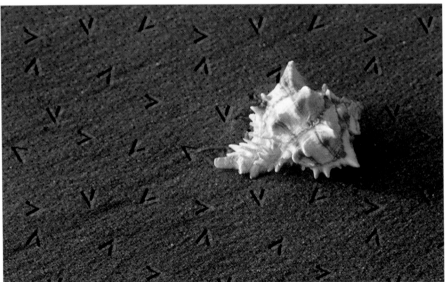

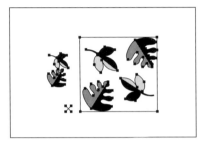

1. Open one of the Patterns and Textures files in Adobe Illustrator, or open your custom pattern file. Select a pattern tile and copy it to the Clipboard. Create a new file, and paste the pattern tile into the new file.

2. If desired, change the colors in the pattern tile. Note that because the pattern tiles from Collectors Edition are grouped, you must use the direct-selection tool to select individual objects in the tile.

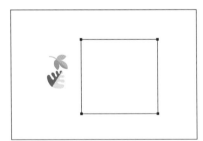

3. For Adobe Photoshop to import the tile correctly, you will need to create crop marks around the pattern tile. Select the bounding box rectangle, and copy it to the Clipboard. Deselect everything (Shift+⌘+A), and then choose Edit > Paste in Front (⌘F). The rectangle is pasted over the pattern artwork.

4. With the rectangle still selected, choose Object > Make > Cropmarks. Save the file.

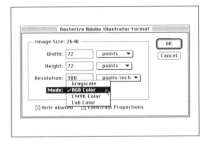

5. In Photoshop, open the Illustrator file you just saved. If you plan to use the pattern tile with other Photoshop files, be sure to open the file in the same mode as those files. Photoshop won't allow you to use a pattern defined in one mode in a file of a different mode. If your pattern contains only stripes or plaids at 90° angles, deselect the Anti-aliased option.

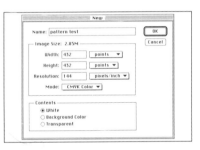

6. Select the entire tile artwork, and choose Edit > Define Pattern. The pattern tile is now temporarily stored in memory. It will be erased if another pattern is defined or when you quit Photoshop.

7. Choose File > Save As, and save the tile with a different name from the Illustrator tile name. (Choosing Save will replace the Illustrator file.) Create a new file that is large enough to contain multiple pattern tiles. Be sure to open the new file in the same mode as the pattern tile.

8. Now test the pattern tile. Choose Edit > Fill, and select Pattern from the Use pop-up menu.

9. Check the overall pattern for texture and color balance. If you are satisfied with the test, the pattern is ready to use. If you want to apply the pattern to an existing image, continue with step 10.

10. Open the file you want to add the pattern to, and select the area you want to fill.

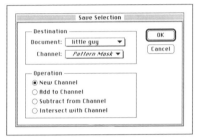

11. You will mask the pattern on a new layer so that you can easily experiment with different effects. Open the Layers palette, and create a new layer. Name it *pattern*.

12. With the selection still active, choose Select > Save Selection. Choose *Pattern Mask* from the Channel pop-up menu. This saves the selection as a layer mask on the pattern layer.

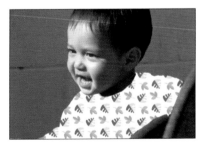

13. Click the pattern layer thumbnail in the Layers palette. Fill the layer with your pattern.

14. If you want to blend the pattern with the underlying image, experiment with the different modes in the Layers palette. For a more subtle effect, reduce the opacity. In this example, we used Saturation mode, which changed the shirt and pattern colors.

Shading with lines

Software needed: Adobe Illustrator 5.5, Adobe Collector's Edition: Patterns & Textures

This is a modern version of a very old technique used to add textures to simple drawings. To create this effect, you first create a simple posterized drawing with different tones of one color. Then, instead of filling the posterized tones with different colors, you fill each shape with a line pattern. To enhance the effect, you can scale and rotate the line patterns to fit their shapes. The first method in this technique shows how to reproduce tonal variations using different patterns and rotations. The second method shows how to reproduce different tonal variations using crosshatching. See the chart at the left for other variations on this technique.

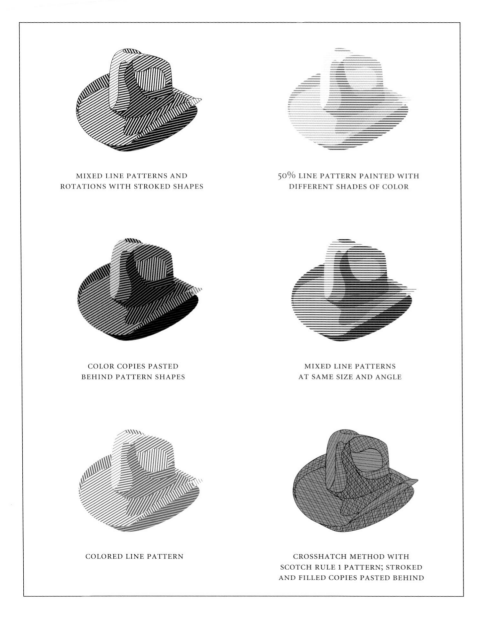

MIXED LINE PATTERNS AND
ROTATIONS WITH STROKED SHAPES

50% LINE PATTERN PAINTED WITH
DIFFERENT SHADES OF COLOR

COLOR COPIES PASTED
BEHIND PATTERN SHAPES

MIXED LINE PATTERNS
AT SAME SIZE AND ANGLE

COLORED LINE PATTERN

CROSSHATCH METHOD WITH
SCOTCH RULE 1 PATTERN; STROKED
AND FILLED COPIES PASTED BEHIND

Tone matching method

1. Create a posterized illustration with simplified shapes that define the tonal areas in the image. For instructions on creating posterized illustrations, see pages 80–81.

2. For this technique, you will need to open two pattern files. Open the Line Patterns folder in the Adobe Collector's Edition folder located on the Adobe Illustrator CD-ROM, and open *Lines 10 lpi 10-60%* and *Lines 10 lpi 70-90%*. Keep these files open until you have painted all the shapes with patterns.

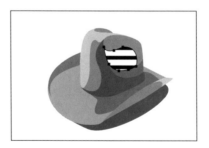

3. Return to the illustration file. Select one of the shapes, and note the percentage of the fill color. Then click the pattern icon in the Paint Style palette, and select the line pattern with the same tint percentage. In this example, we selected the pattern *10 lpi-40%* to fill a shape that was 40% black. Don't worry about the size of the pattern; you'll scale the pattern in a later step.

4. Continue filling each toned shape with its corresponding pattern tone until all shapes in the image have been filled.

58

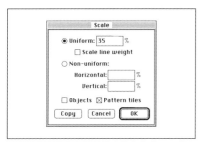

5. If desired, scale the patterns to fit the shapes they fill. To scale just the patterns within the shapes, select the shapes, and double-click the scale tool. Deselect the Objects option; this selects the Pattern Tiles option. Enter the desired scale percentage, and click OK. You can also scale just the pattern by holding down the P key and dragging with the scale tool.

6. Once the patterns have been scaled, evaluate the patterns to determine whether they create enough contrast between shapes. You may want to select a pattern with a different tint percentage within some of the shapes to make them darker or lighter.

7. You can also create contrast between shapes by rotating the patterns at different angles. To do this, first select the shape or shapes that you want to alter.

8. To rotate just the patterns within the shapes, select the shapes, and double-click the rotate tool. Deselect the Objects option; this selects the Pattern Tiles option. Enter the desired rotation angle, and click OK. You can also rotate just the pattern by holding down the P key and dragging with the rotate tool.

9. Continue rotating the patterns within the shapes until the effect is as you want it. Then save the file.

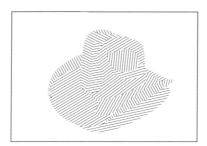

Crosshatch method

1. You can also create contrast between shapes by overlapping patterns at different angles. Follow steps 1 through 5 of the previous method using a line pattern with a transparent background. In this example, we filled all the shapes with the same pattern but at different angles.

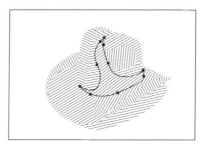

2. Select one of the shapes representing a darker tone in the illustration. Copy it to the Clipboard, and paste the copy in front of the selection (⌘F).

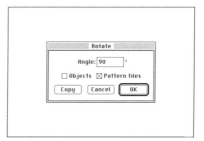

3. Double-click the rotate tool in the toolbox. Deselect the Objects option, and enter 90°. Click OK to rotate the copy on top of the original.

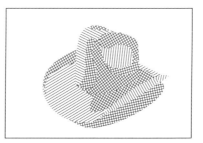

4. Continue to copy and rotate the pattern in each shape that represents a darker tone. The image now has two tones: a light tone, represented by the single lines, and a dark tone, represented by the crosshatching.

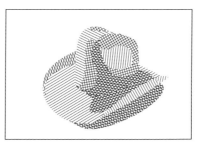

5. To add a third or darker tone, repeat steps 2 and 3 for the shapes representing the darker tones. Add a third copy of the line pattern to these shapes, and rotate the pattern to 45°.

Embellishing three-dimensional graphics

Software needed: Adobe Photoshop 3.0; Adobe Illustrator 4 or later or Adobe Dimensions 2.0

You can use the new Overlay mode in the Layers palette of Adobe Photoshop 3.0 to easily add photographic or painterly textures to graphics created in Adobe Illustrator or Adobe Dimensions. To do this, you simply place the Illustrator or Dimensions graphic onto a layer in Photoshop. You then copy a texture onto an adjacent layer and combine the two layers using Overlay mode. This technique shows how to add a texture to three-dimensional graphics and then adjust the texture to enhance the 3-D effect.

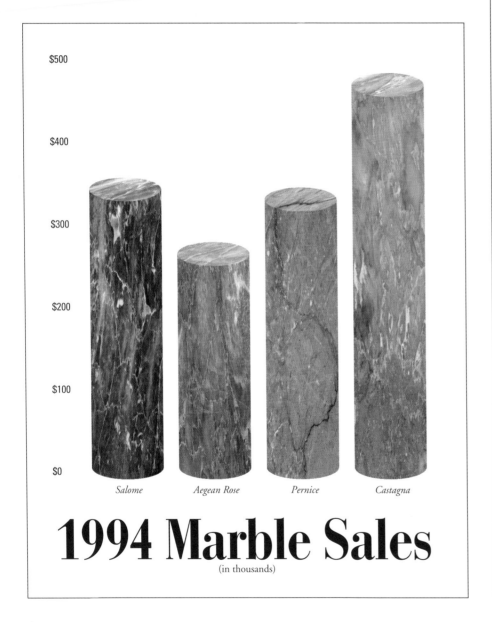

$500

$400

$300

$200

$100

$0

Salome   Aegean Rose   Pernice   Castagna

1994 Marble Sales
(in thousands)

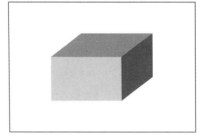

1. Create a three-dimensional shape in Adobe Illustrator or Adobe Dimensions. For the best results, paint the shape with shades of black only. Use 50% black or more for shadow areas. Areas of the shape filled with 50% black will show 100% of the texture in the final artwork; areas filled with 100% black or white will not be affected. Save the file.

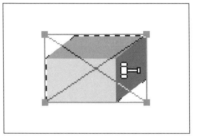

2. Create a new file in Adobe Photoshop at the size and resolution you want for the final image. Choose File > Place to place the graphics you created in step 1. Position and scale the placed artwork as desired; then click with the hammer icon to rasterize the graphics.

3. Open a Photoshop file with a texture that you want to appear on the surface of the three-dimensional shape. Select the area of texture that you want to use. Adjust the windows so that you can see both the texture file and the file with the shape.

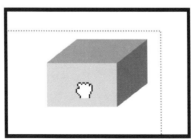

4. Use the move tool to drag the selection from the texture file window into the graphics file window.

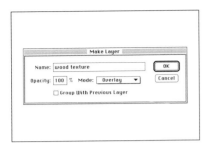

5. Now double-click the floating selection in the Layers palette, choose Overlay from the Mode menu, and click OK.

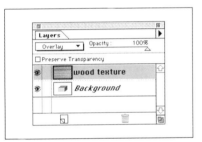

6. Because the new layer is set to Overlay mode, the texture shows through only areas of the graphic that contain percentages of black. Areas filled with 100% black or 100% white are unaffected. If you are satisfied with the result, save the file and skip to step 9. If you want to add a new textured shape to the image, continue with step 7.

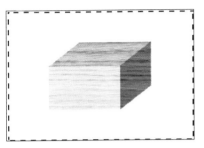

7. Before you add a new texture and shape to the file, you will group the current texture and shape layers so that the texture does not affect any other layers below it. Hold down the Option/Alt key, and click the line between the layers you want to group. The line between the two layers is replaced by a dotted line.

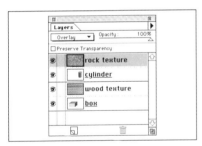

8. Repeat steps 1–7 for each new shape. Rename the shape layers so that the names correspond to the shapes they contain. Be sure to group each texture with its corresponding shape.

9. Evaluate the image to determine whether the texture on the top or sides of the graphics need adjustments to create a three-dimensional effect. In this example, the wood grain on the side of the cylinder is at the wrong angle, and the top of the cylinder needs to be scaled to add perspective.

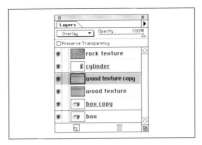

10. To adjust the texture in the sides of your graphics, first make a copy of the two layers associated with the graphic you want to adjust. Drag each layer name down to the New Layer icon. Because these layers are part of a group, the copies appear directly above the original layers and within the same group.

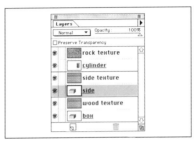

11. Now move the copied layers above their original group. You will need to group each texture with its corresponding shape. Rename the layer copies *side* and *side texture*.

12. Select the side layer, and make a selection of the side. You can use the selection tools to do this, or (to avoid redrawing the path) you can copy and paste the path from the original Illustrator file. Note that copying and pasting works only if you did not scale the object when you placed it in step 2.

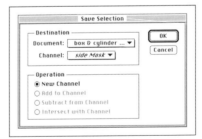

13. To isolate the side of the object, you will create a layer mask. With the side layer still the active layer, choose Select > Save Selection. Choose *side Mask* from the Channel pop-up menu. Deselect (⌘/Ctrl+D).

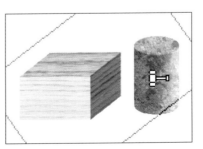

14. Now adjust the texture as desired. Select the side texture layer in the Layers palette. To rotate the texture, choose Image > Rotate > Free, and drag the corner handles of the box. When you are satisfied with the results, click inside the box.

15. If desired, reposition the texture. With the texture layer still active, select the move tool and drag to adjust the texture. When you are satisfied with the results, save the file. If the top of one of the shapes needs adjustment, continue with step 16.

20. Reposition the texture if needed; then deselect (⌘/Ctrl+D). When you are satisfied with the results, save the file.

16. To adjust the texture in the tops of your graphics, first repeat steps 10 and 11 to make duplicates of the shape layer and its texture layer. Rename these duplicate layers *top* and *top texture*. Position them just above their original group and regroup the layers as necessary.

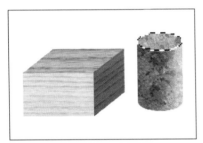

17. Make the top layer the active layer, and select the top of the graphic.

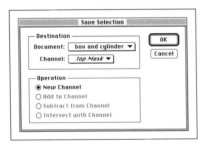

18. To isolate the top of the object, you will create a layer mask. With the top layer still the active layer, choose Select > Save Selection. Choose *top Mask* from the Channel pop-up menu. Deselect (⌘/Ctrl+D).

19. Now adjust the texture as desired. Select the top texture layer in the Layers palette. To scale the texture vertically, choose Image > Effects > Scale, and drag the corner handles of the box straight up. When you are satisfied with the effect, click inside the box.

5 Text Effects

Glowing text

Software needed: Photoshop 3.0, Adobe Type Manager, Type 1 fonts

To create glowing text, you create a border selection and then apply the Gaussian Blur filter. The size of the border and the amount you blur it varies with the typeface and type size you use. The chart at the left shows some examples of different type styles and weights with different border, feather, and blurring amounts. For the best results, use large sans serif typefaces with this technique and avoid delicate script typefaces.

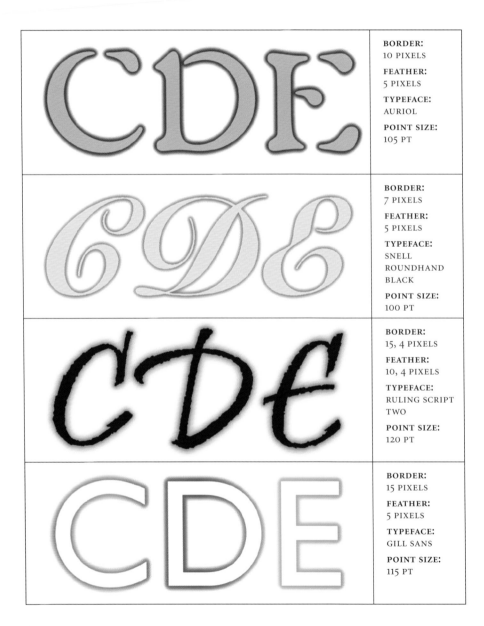

BORDER: 10 PIXELS	
FEATHER: 5 PIXELS	
TYPEFACE: AURIOL	
POINT SIZE: 105 PT	

BORDER: 7 PIXELS	
FEATHER: 5 PIXELS	
TYPEFACE: SNELL ROUNDHAND BLACK	
POINT SIZE: 100 PT	

BORDER: 15, 4 PIXELS	
FEATHER: 10, 4 PIXELS	
TYPEFACE: RULING SCRIPT TWO	
POINT SIZE: 120 PT	

BORDER: 15 PIXELS	
FEATHER: 5 PIXELS	
TYPEFACE: GILL SANS	
POINT SIZE: 115 PT	

1. Open the color image or new RGB document that you want to create text in. Because the type should be on a transparent layer, create a new layer for the type, and name it *type.*

2. Use the type tool to enter the text you want on the type layer. Make sure that you are using Adobe Type Manager and that the Anti-aliased option in the Type dialog box is selected. Depending on how thick you want the glow, add space between the letters to keep them from running together after you add the glow. Click OK.

3. Position the text as you want it, and fill it with the desired color.

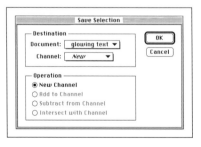

4. Click the selection icon in the Channels palette to save the selection to a new channel. You will use this selection later.

5. Now create another layer, and name it *type glow.*

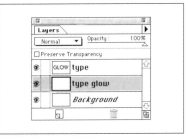

6. Move the type glow layer directly below the type layer. Option/Alt-click the channel in the Channels palette to load the selection.

7. Now you will create the glow. Choose Select > Modify > Border. Enter a border width, and click OK.

8. The Border command straddles the edges of the selection and creates a selection border that is half inside and half outside the type. If necessary, choose Edit > Undo (⌘/Ctrl+Z) and experiment with the border width until you get the size you want for your typeface. In this example, we used a border width of 8 pixels for 45-point Kabel bold type.

9. Select the foreground color you want to use for the glow, and then press Option+Delete (Macintosh) or Alt+Backspace (Windows) to fill the area. Deselect everything (⌘/Ctrl+D).

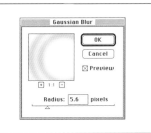

10. With the type glow layer still selected, choose Filter > Blur > Gaussian Blur. This filter softens the edge of the glow. Use the Preview option to determine the blur radius you want. Then click OK.

11. If you are satisfied with this glow, save the file.

Variation 1: For a brighter glow, duplicate the type glow layer by dragging the layer to the New Layer icon in the Layers palette. The second glow layer increases the intensity of the glow.

Variation 2: To bring the glow both inside and outside the type, drag the type glow layer directly above the type layer in the Layers palette.

Variation 3: If you want a glow on the inside of the type only, drag the type glow layer directly above the type layer; then load the type selection by Option/Alt-clicking the channel in the Channels palette. With the type glow layer active, choose Select > Save Selection, and choose *type glow Mask* as the Channel. This creates a layer mask that hides the glow outside the type.

Shadowed text

Software needed: Adobe Photoshop 3.0, Adobe Type Manager, Type 1 Fonts

Drop shadows for text, like glowing text outlines, are best created using layers. In this procedure, you duplicate the type layer to create the shadow and then apply the Gaussian Blur filter to soften the edges. As with glowing text outlines, the values you use in this procedure depend in part on the font you are using. Delicate typefaces at small point sizes require less blurring than heavy faces at large sizes. If your final output is film and you want the shadow to be a color other than black, check with your service bureau; some service bureaus prefer black drop shadows to avoid printing and registration problems.

1. Open the background image that you want to use. Then open the Layers palette, create a new layer, and name it *type*.

2. Create the type on the new layer. You can create the type in Adobe Photoshop using the type tool, or you can create the type in Adobe Illustrator and then use Photoshop's Place command to import the type.

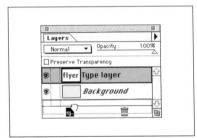

3. In the Layers palette, drag the type layer down to the New Layer icon to create a duplicate of the layer. Double-click the new layer, and name it *type shadow*.

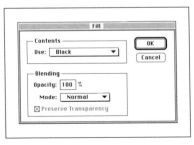

4. Turn on the Preserve Transparency option for the type shadow layer so that you can modify only the contents of the layer. Choose Edit > Fill, or click Fill in the Commands palette. Fill the shadow with the color you want.

5. Turn off the Preserve Transparency option. Move the shadow so that it is slightly offset from the type. In this example, we moved the shadow down and to the right using the arrow keys.

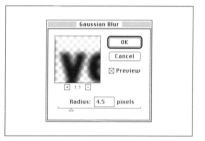

6. Select the type shadow layer in the Layers palette, and drag it below the type layer. This places the shadow behind the type.

7. Now use the Gaussian Blur filter to soften the edges of the shadow. With the type shadow layer still selected, choose Filter > Blur > Gaussian Blur. Use the Preview option to help determine the best amount to blur the shadow; then click OK.

8. To further soften the effect of the shadow, adjust its opacity in the Layers palette.

Variation: For a different effect, choose a color other than black in step 4, and then select the Multiply mode in the Layers palette. Using Multiply mode allows the texture of the background to show through the shadow. Depending on the color you use, you may want to adjust the opacity of the shadow.

❧ *Creating an editable lens flare*

In photography, a lens flare is caused by the refraction of light inside a camera lens. This technique shows how to create a digital lens flare that you can easily move around an image and modify without affecting the underlying image.

Open a Photoshop file that you want to apply the lens flare effect to.

Create a new layer, and name it *lens flare*. Set its mode to Screen, select the Fill with Screen Neutral Color option. Click OK.

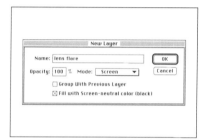

With the lens flare layer still selected, choose Filter > Render > Lens Flare. Click to position the flare center, select the lens type, and set the desired brightness. In this example we used a Brightness value of 139 and the 50–300 mm zoom lens type. Click OK.

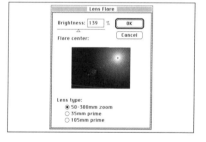

To soften the effect, adjust the opacity of the lens flare layer. You can also create some interesting effects by adjusting the highlights using the Curves dialog box (⌘/Ctrl+M).

Translucent shapes

Software needed: Adobe Photoshop 3.0

This simple technique shows how to create semitransparent text containers, so that columns of text can be added to an Adobe Photoshop image without obscuring the artwork underneath. Once you create the shape in Adobe Photoshop, you can place the file in Adobe Illustrator, Adobe PageMaker™, or any other drawing or page layout program. Using the Layers palette in Adobe Photoshop 3.0 makes it easy to modify the text container at any time without affecting any other image components. You can also use this technique to create translucent type or other shape that can be drawn or placed over an Adobe Photoshop image .

Cornfields have come to symbolize the idyllic youth of rural midwesterners. At the height of the corn season in Kazaquan, Minnesota, small farmers still rely on their even smaller counterparts for help with the harvest. In spite of drastic changes in agriculture in the past 50 years, over 60 percent of the productive farm land in Ohio, Michigan, Indiana, and Minnesota, is owned by small, family-owned farming operations. And at the height [continued on page 96]

by O. B. Tarwarter

1. Open the image in which you want the translucent shape. If you are creating a text container that you will use in a page layout program, record the exact size and placement of the shape that you need in the page layout program.

2. Create a new layer, and name it *shape.*

3. With the new layer active, create the shape. For a precise rectangle or circle, double-click the marquee tool and enter the dimensions you want in the dialog box. You can also use type or other objects placed from the Adobe Illustrator program.

4. Select a light color to fill the selection. (White or cream work best if you plan to add text to the area.) To make the shape blend in with the image, use the eyedropper tool to sample a color from the image. Press Option+Delete (Macintosh) or Alt+Backspace (Windows) to fill the selection with the selected color. Then deselect (⌘/Ctrl+D).

5. Use the opacity slider in the Layers palette to adjust the opacity of the fill.

6. If the shape needs repositioning, select the move tool, and move the shape to the desired position.

7. To change the color of the shape, select the color you want, click Preserve Transparency in the Layers palette, and press Option+Delete (Macintosh) or Alt+Backspace (Windows) to fill the shape. Adjust the opacity if desired.

8. Choose File > Save a Copy and save a flattened version of the file in EPS format. The Save a Copy command lets you save a flattened version of the file in another format in a single step and without affecting the current file.

9. Place the image in your drawing or page layout program, and then add the text.

❧ Moving the selection marquee

To move a selection marquee without affecting the image, hold down Command and Option (Macintosh) or Ctrl and Alt (Windows), and drag the selection into position. This moves the selection marquee without moving the contents of the selection. Hold down the Shift key as you drag to constrain the movement to the nearest 45-degree angle.

❧ Adobe Photoshop Quick Keys

KEYSTROKES	RESULT
/	*Turns Preserve Transparency on and off for the active layer*
[	*Sets brush size to next larger size*
]	*Sets brush size to next smaller size*
{	*Sets brush size to first brush*
}	*Sets brush size to last brush*
Return	*Activates the current tool's options palette. If the palette is already active, highlights the first text box.*
Enter + Active path	*If a painting tool is active, strokes the path with that tool. Otherwise, closes the path (if open), and converts it to a selection.*
1–0	*If a painting tool is active, changes opacity to 10 times the number (or to 100 for 'o'). If any other tool is active, changes the opacity of the active selection or layer.*
Up Arrow and Down Arrow	*When a number text box is active, increase and decrease the value by one unit. Shift + Arrow key bump the value by 10 units.*
⌘/Ctrl+[	*Selects the next visible layer down the layer stack.**
⌘/Ctrl+Option/Alt+[	*Selects the bottom layer.**
⌘/Ctrl+]	*Selects the next visible layer up the layer stack.**
⌘/Ctrl+Option/Alt+]	*Selects the top layer.**
⌘/Ctrl+Option/Alt+(+)	*Zoom in to 16:1*
⌘/Ctrl+Option/Alt+(-)	*Zooms down to 1:16*

*If only one layer is visible, these shortcuts cycle through the Layers palette, making layers visible one at a time.

Recessed text

Software needed: Adobe Photoshop 3.0

This technique shows how to create the inverse effect of the embossing technique on page 76. Because you must create the edges of the recessed type manually, however, the procedure is somewhat more involved. To make type look like it recedes into a textured surface, you must create edges that differentiate the top surface of the type from the recessed surface. To do this, you use two selection channels to define the edge of the type. The final file is composed of four layers. Using layers gives you the ability to experiment with different surfaces and opacity amounts for the shadows and highlights.

1. Open the texture file in which you want the recessed text. Light to medium-light colored textures give the best results because the recessed image is more visible in the final artwork.

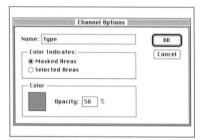

2. Create a new channel, and name it *type*. Click OK.

3. Add the type to this channel. You can create the type in Photoshop or bring the type in from Adobe Illustrator. Fill the type with white.

4. Reselect the RGB channel in the Channels palette. Create a new layer, and name it *recessed type*.

5. If the type selection is not still active, load the selection by Option/Alt-clicking the type channel in the Channels palette. Make sure that the recessed type layer is still active, and fill the type selection with 100% black.

6. Deselect the type (⌘/Ctrl+D), and lower the opacity setting on the recessed type layer. In this example, we reduced the opacity to 30%.

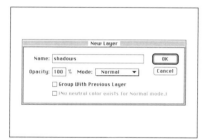

7. Create a new layer, and name it *shadows*. This layer will contain two shadows: a soft cast shadow and an edge shadow.

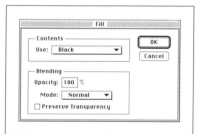

8. Fill the shadows layer with 100% black. The layer will temporarily cover up the background image.

9. Option/Alt-click the type channel to load the selection. Delete the black fill from that selection area, and then deselect the type (⌘/Ctrl+D).

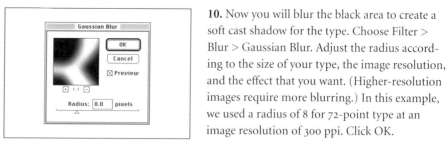

10. Now you will blur the black area to create a soft cast shadow for the type. Choose Filter > Blur > Gaussian Blur. Adjust the radius according to the size of your type, the image resolution, and the effect that you want. (Higher-resolution images require more blurring.) In this example, we used a radius of 8 for 72-point type at an image resolution of 300 ppi. Click OK.

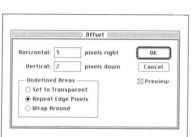

11. Next you will offset the shadow slightly to push it inside the type. Choose Filter > Other > Offset. Offset the selection in the direction that you want the shadow to fall. In this example, we pushed the shadow down and to the right to create the effect of a light source in the upper left of the image. Make sure that the Repeat Edge Pixels option is selected, and click OK.

12. Option/Alt-click the type channel to load the selection. Choose Select > Inverse, and delete the remaining black in the image. Deselect the type (⌘/Ctrl+D), and then duplicate the type channel by dragging it down to the New Channel icon in the Channels palette. Double-click the channel, and name it *highlight edge*. You will use this channel to select the highlights.

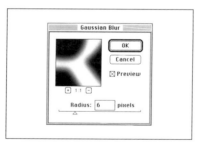

13. Soften the highlight edge channel by choosing Filter > Blur > Gaussian Blur and entering a slightly smaller value than you used in step 10. In this example, we used a radius of 6 pixels. Click OK.

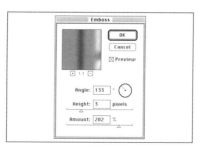

14. Now you will create an embossed version of the image to help isolate the edges of the type. Choose Filter > Stylize > Emboss. Click Preview, and experiment with different settings until you have a strong black and white in the image. Make sure that the angle causes the black in the embossed letters to appear over the shadow you offset in step 11. Click OK.

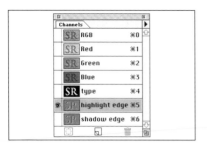

15. Duplicate the highlight edge channel by dragging the channel down to the New Channel icon in the Channels palette. Double-click the new channel, and name it *shadow edge*. You will use this same image to isolate the shadow edges later in the procedure. Reselect the highlight edge channel.

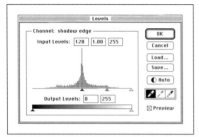

16. Choose Image > Adjust > Levels (⌘/Ctrl+L). Enter 128 in the Input Levels shadow box, and click OK. This fills all areas in the channel with black except the highlight edges.

17. Now you will clean up the edges of the highlight to make them crisp and sharp. Option/Alt-click the type channel to load the selection into the highlight edge channel. Fill the selection with 100% black.

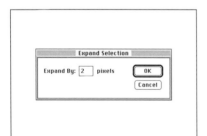

18. Choose Select > Modify > Expand. Expand the selection slightly. The number of pixels you choose defines the width of the highlight edges. In this example, we used a value of 2 pixels.

19. Now choose Select > Inverse, and fill the selection with black to isolate the highlight edges. Deselect (⌘/Ctrl+D).

20. Now select the shadow edge channel in the Channels palette. Invert the channel (⌘/Ctrl+I), and then repeat steps 16-19 to isolate the shadow edges. You now have the three channels you need to create the shadows and highlights for the recessed type.

21. Reselect the RGB channel. Create a new layer, and name it *highlight edge*.

22. Option/Alt-click the highlight edge channel in the Channels palette to load the selection onto the new layer.

23. With the new layer still selected, fill the selection with white. Deselect (⌘/Ctrl+D), and lower the opacity for that layer. In this example, we reduced the opacity to 50%.

24. Now select the shadows layer in the Layers palette, and Option/Alt-click the shadow edge channel to load the selection. Fill the selection with 100% black, and deselect (⌘/Ctrl+D). If desired, adjust the opacity of the different layers in the image to soften or harden the effect. If necessary, use the airbrush tool with a very small brush to touch up the edges.

Special Effects

Filter combinations

Software needed: Adobe Photoshop 2.0

Sometimes you want a texture or special effect that can't be achieved with the application of just one filter. Shown here are just a few of the hundreds of combinations you can use to enhance Adobe Photoshop images. Although these examples illustrate filters applied to the entire image, these combinations can also be applied to just a selected area. To create an effect shown here, apply the filters in the order indicated. Note, however, that the effect may vary with different image resolutions and modes. The images here are CMYK files at a resolution of 200 pixels per inch.

ORIGINAL

1. GAUSSIAN BLUR: 2.0
2. DIFFUSE: NORMAL, TWO TIMES

1. FIND EDGES
2. FACET

1. CRYSTALLIZE: 7.0
2. FIND EDGES

1. MOSAIC: 10
2. RIPPLE: 100, MEDIUM

1. POINTILLIZE: 5
2. FACET: THREE TIMES

1. HIGH PASS: 10
2. DIFFUSE: LIGHTEN ONLY, THREE TIMES

1. GAUSSIAN BLUR: 2.0
2. DIFFUSE: NORMAL, TWO TIMES

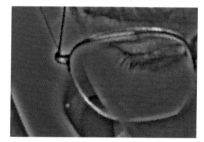

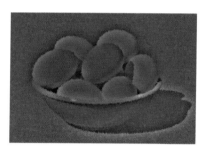

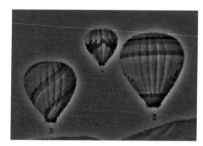

Embossing

Software needed: Adobe Photoshop 3.0, Adobe Illustrator 4 or later (optional)

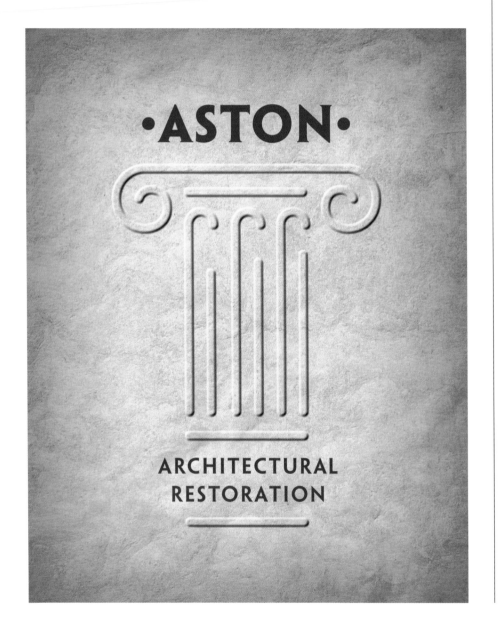

Adobe Photoshop's Emboss filter creates the illusion of raised edges by filling an object with gray and then using the original fill color to create borders around the object. This technique shows how to finesse the edges of an embossed object to give it a more realistic look. In reality, an embossed object often has a harder edge around the base of the object, while the surface edges of the object retain a softer, molded look. To get this effect, you first blur the object before embossing; after embossing, you re-outline the base of the object using the background fill color or texture.

1. In Adobe Photoshop, create a surface for your embossed graphics. For the best results, use a textured surface.

2. Open the Layers palette, and create a new layer. Name the new layer after your embossed image.

3. To fill the layer with white, choose Edit > Fill (Shift+Delete/Backspace), and choose White from the Use pop-up menu. Make sure that the Opacity is 100% and the Mode is Normal; then click OK.

4. Add the type or graphic to the new layer, and fill it with black. You can copy and paste images and type directly from Adobe Illustrator; if you do, fill the graphic with black before you bring it into Photoshop. Remember that the Emboss filter uses the fill color of the object to create the raised edges.

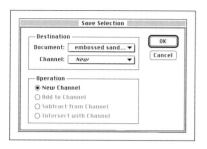

5. While the type or graphic is still selected, choose Select > Save Selection or use the Channels palette to save the selection to a new channel. You will need to use the selection later in this procedure. Save the file so that you can revert to this step if you don't like the final effect.

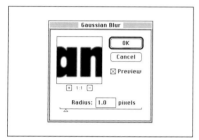

6. Deselect everything (⌘/Ctrl+D), and choose Filter > Blur > Gaussian Blur. Choose an amount that will soften the edges of the type or graphic. The amount you should choose depends on the resolution of your image and the texture of your background. A high-resolution image requires more blurring than a low-resolution image.

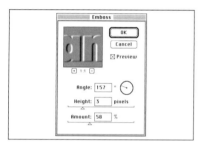

7. Choose Filter > Stylize > Emboss. You may need to adjust the angle to suit the angles in the letterforms. To create a more pronounced effect, increase the Height; to create more contrast, increase the Amount. The Amount you use should result in light and dark grays in the image rather than black and white.

8. Examine the results. If you are satisfied with the effect, skip to step 14. If you want to sharpen the outer edges of the object, continue with step 9.

9. Load the selection from the channel you created in step 5 by Option/Alt-clicking the channel name in the Channels palette.

10. Now choose Select > Modify > Expand to enlarge the selection slightly. Enter an amount that is smaller than the Height you used in step 7. Different amounts will produce different effects; experiment until you are satisfied with the results.

11. Choose Select > Inverse to select the background.

12. Hide the selection (⌘/Ctrl+H). Then use the eyedropper tool to sample the color of the background.

13. Press Option+Delete (Macintosh) or Alt+Backspace (Windows) to fill the selection. This step outlines the edges of the selection with the background color and creates a cleaner, crisper look. Deselect everything (⌘/Ctrl+D).

14. To combine the embossed graphics with the background texture, choose the Hard Light mode for the embossed layer in the Layers palette. Try the Soft Light mode or lower the transparency for a more subtle effect. If you want to re-emboss the image, choose File > Revert and then begin again with step 6.

Posterizing photographs

Software needed: Adobe Photoshop 3.0

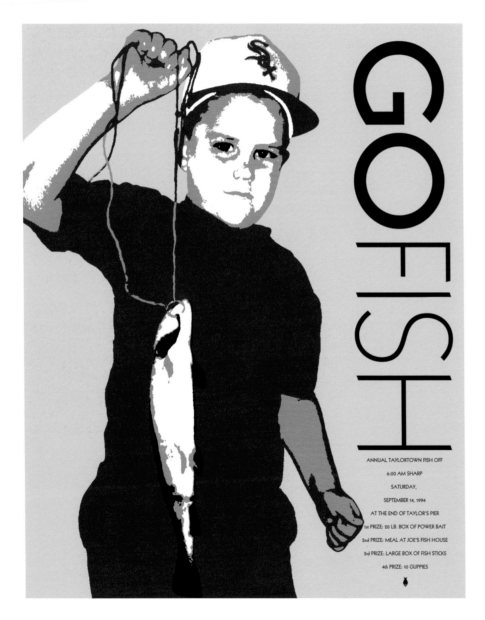

If you've used the Adobe Photoshop Posterize command to posterize color images, you've probably produced some unexpected results. This is because Photoshop posterizes each channel of a color image. That means that a two-level posterization produces two colors in each channel of an image, generating a total of eight colors in an RGB image (2 × 2 × 2) and 16 colors in a CMYK image. The technique described here provides an alternative way to create color posterizations that gives you more control over the number of colors as well as the colors themselves. This procedure lends itself well to process or custom color inks.

1. Open the file you want to posterize. Crop the file to the size and resolution you want. If the file is a color file, choose Image > Adjust > Desaturate.

2. Choose Image > Duplicate. Enter a filename, click OK, and close the original file. This leaves the original file intact on disk so that you can freely experiment with different colors and levels of posterization.

3. Choose Image > Map > Posterize. Click Preview, and enter the number of colors you think you want in your poster. When you have the effect you want, click OK. If you need to adjust the contrast in the image to retain detail, click Cancel, adjust the image and then repeat this step. (See "Correcting Problem Areas in Posterizations" at the end of this technique.)

4. Now you will remove any unwanted detail or awkward shapes from your image. Select the paintbrush tool; then hold down Option/Alt and use the eyedropper to select a gray in the image that you want to paint with. Paint over the unwanted areas. In this example, we removed several specks of white from the image.

5. If you started with a grayscale image, convert the image to RGB mode. Then double-click the magic wand tool, set the Tolerance to 0, and deselect the Anti-aliased option. These options tell the magic wand tool to select only pixels with exactly the same color value as the pixel you click.

6. Click one of the black areas in the image; then choose Select > Similar to select all black in the image.

7. Select the color that you want to fill the darkest areas of the image, and press Option+Delete (Macintosh) or Alt+Backspace (Windows) to fill the selection. To hide the selection marquee, choose Select > Hide Edges.

8. Now use the magic wand tool to select the next darkest level of gray, and choose Select > Similar again.

9. Fill the selection with the color you want for this gray level. Repeat steps 8 and 9 for each remaining gray level in your image. If you need to resize the file after posterizing, be sure to change the Interpolation method in the Preferences dialog box to Nearest Neighbor. This prevents anti-aliasing, which adds new gray levels to the file.

∾ Correcting problem areas in posterizations

Because posterizing an image reduces the number of gray levels in the image, key areas in an image may lose so much detail that they blend into other areas. By using the Preview option in the Posterize dialog box, you can figure out the number of levels that gives you the results you want as well as identify problem areas in an image. You can then correct the brightness and contrast in those areas before you posterize.

For example, the image shown here has been posterized to four levels instead of the three used in the preceding technique. Compare this image to the one shown in step 4. Notice that the extra posterization level has caused the man's face to disappear. To get good results using four levels, we must first adjust the contrast in this area of the image.

To do this, we first selected the problem area in the image. We then used Curves (⌘M) to increase the contrast in the area.

We then reapplied the Posterize command using four levels. Notice that the man's face now retains its detail and doesn't blend into the sweater.

∾ Building a color palette for color posterization

When colorizing a posterized image, it's helpful to build a color palette for the image before you start. To do this, open the Swatch palette and use the eyedropper to sample each of the gray levels in the grayscale image. Drag the pointer to a blank swatch in the Swatch palette and click to fill the swatch, or hold down Shift+⌘/Ctrl and click to replace an existing swatch. Then fill the swatch below each gray in the palette with the color you will use to replace the gray.

Posterize-style illustrations

Software needed: Adobe Photoshop 2.5 or later, Adobe Illustrator 4 or later

This technique shows how to create a very stylized illustration from a photograph. Reminiscent of early 20th century German poster art, the drawings are made up of flat, simplified shapes and lend themselves well to printing with custom colors. To create the illustration, you start with an existing photograph, simplify it, and trace it in Photoshop using the pen tool. You then copy the paths into Illustrator and paint them. Although you can use Adobe Streamline to produce posterized illustrations automatically, this technique and a little drawing ability will give you the best results.

1. Open the Adobe Photoshop file you want to use as a basis for your illustration. If the file is a color file, convert it to Grayscale mode. You will first posterize this image so that you can more easily use it as a template for your pen tool shapes. Posterizing the image simplifies it and breaks up its different tonal areas into distinct shapes.

2. Choose Image > Map > Posterize, and click the Preview option. Experiment with different numbers of levels, and evaluate the shapes in the image. If you like the effect of the posterization and you're not losing too much detail in the image, click OK and skip to step 5. If important details are lost in the preview, click Cancel and continue with step 3.

3. Use Levels (⌘/Ctrl+L) or Curves (⌘/Ctrl+M) to increase the contrast in the areas that are losing detail. For more information on adjusting a Photoshop file for optimal posterization, see page 78.

4. Choose Image > Map > Posterize again, and re-evaluate different posterization levels. If necessary, repeat steps 2 and 3 until the posterized image contains the shapes you need to create your illustration.

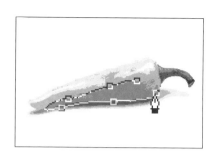

5. Select the pen tool from the Paths palette. Begin to trace the shapes in the image.

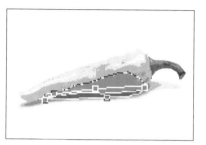

6. As you draw, keep in mind that the shapes will overlap in the Illustrator file. For this reason, you can draw certain edges more roughly than others. In this example, we knew the black shadow shape would be layered behind the shape above it, so we let the upper path of the shadow overlap the front of the pepper.

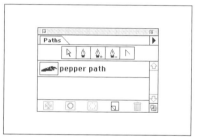

7. Save the paths by double-clicking *Work path* in the Paths palette. If you have more than one subject in the image, you may want to save each set of shapes as separate paths. Name each path after its subject for easy reference.

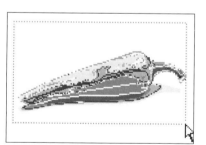

8. Click the selection tool, and drag to select the entire subject. Copy the shapes to the Clipboard.

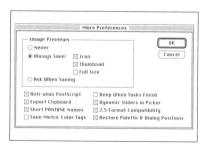

9. If you're using Illustrator 5.0 or later and your computer has enough memory to run Photoshop and Illustrator at the same time, open the General Preferences dialog box (⌘/Ctrl+K), click More, and make sure that the Export Clipboard option is selected. Then skip to step 11. Otherwise, continue with step 10.

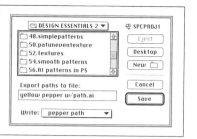

10. To save the paths in Illustrator format, choose File > Export > Paths to Illustrator. Photoshop gives the file the same name as the old file with a suffix *.ai* to indicate that it's an Illustrator file. Save the file.

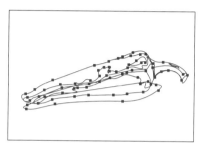

11. Start Adobe Illustrator. If you exported the paths, open the file. If you copied the paths to the Clipboard, paste them into a file.

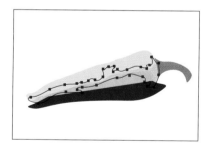

12. Paths brought into Illustrator from Photoshop have no fill and no stroke initially and so are not visible in Preview mode. To help you work with the paths, choose Window > New Window and put the second window in Artwork mode. Resize the windows so that you can preview the results as you paint the shapes in Artwork mode.

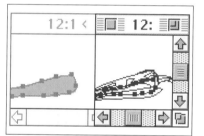

13. If necessary, rearrange the layers as you paint. The layering of the paths is based on the order in which the paths were created. In this example, we brought the selected shape to the front of the artwork.

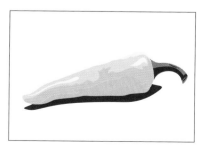

14. Continue filling the shapes with colors. Because the image is now an Illustrator file, the paths can be edited, scaled, and repainted without loss in quality or change in file size. When you are satisfied with the results, save the file.

Creating a textured effect

Software needed: Adobe Photoshop 3.0, Adobe Illustrator 5.5, Adobe Type Manager, Type 1 Fonts

Some artists try to simulate an eroded or weathered effect with type or graphics by making a series of photocopies in which each copy is made from the previous copy. The following technique lets you achieve a similar look with more control and less paper. Use the chart below to figure out how to apply the filter to get the effect you want. Notice that the effect varies dramatically at different resolutions.

DIFFUSE AMOUNT	PHOTOSHOP RESOLUTION (PIXELS PER INCH)		
	100 PPI	200 PPI	300 PPI
NONE	Aa	Aa	Aa
DIFFUSE ONE TIME NORMAL	Aa	Aa	Aa
DIFFUSE TWO TIMES NORMAL	Aa	Aa	Aa
DIFFUSE THREE TIMES NORMAL	Aa	Aa	Aa
DIFFUSE TEN TIMES NORMAL	Aa	Aa	Aa
DIFFUSE TWO TIMES LIGHTEN	Aa	Aa	Aa
DIFFUSE FIVE TIMES LIGHTEN		Aa	Aa
DIFFUSE TWO TIMES DARKEN	Aa	Aa	Aa
DIFFUSE FIVE TIMES DARKEN	Aa	Aa	Aa

1. Create an image using Adobe Illustrator, and paint it as desired. (In general, this effect works best on large display type or graphics.) Save the file.

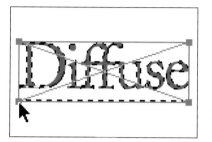

2. Open or create the Adobe Photoshop file you wish to add the eroded graphics to. Create a new layer and name it *diffused*. Choose File > Place, and select the Illustrator file you created in step 1. Photoshop displays the graphic with a box around it; to scale the graphic, drag the corner points.

3. When the size is as you want it, click inside the box to place the file and rasterize the graphic in Photoshop. The placed image appears as an active floating selection. Deselect the graphic (⌘/Ctrl+D).

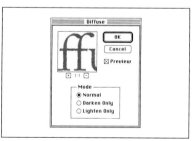

4. Choose Filter > Stylize > Diffuse; then select the Mode option you want (see the chart on the facing page for examples). Using the Lighten Only option creates the effect of the image dissolving; using the Darken Only option creates the effect of the image spreading. Click OK.

5. Depending on the intensity of the effect you want, reapply the filter (⌘/Ctrl+F). (We applied the filter three times.) When you are satisfied with the results, save the file.

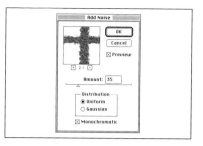

Enhancement 1: You can use the Add Noise filter to add texture to the inner areas of the graphic that are less diffused. Choose Filter > Noise > Add Noise. Select Monochromatic, Uniform, and enter an Amount (we used 35).

Click OK when you are satisfied with the results. Then save the file.

Enhancement 2: You can also use the Add Noise filter with a layer mask to add a texture to the graphic. A background image or flat color will show through this texture. Select the diffused layer, then choose Add Layer Mask from the palette pop-up menu.

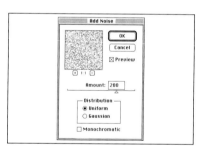

With the layer mask selected, choose Filter > Noise > Add Noise. Select the Uniform option, and enter an Amount (we used 150). The black areas of the mask allow the background to show through the graphic, the white areas mask out the background, and the gray areas create a semi-transparent mask. Click OK when you are satisfied with the amount of texture.

Experiment with different colored backgrounds for different effects. When you are satisfied with the results, choose File > Save a Copy to save a flattened version of the file. Using Save a Copy enables you to save a flattened version of the file in another file format, such as EPS, in one step and without affecting your layered file.

Composite photographs

Software needed: Adobe Photoshop 3.0

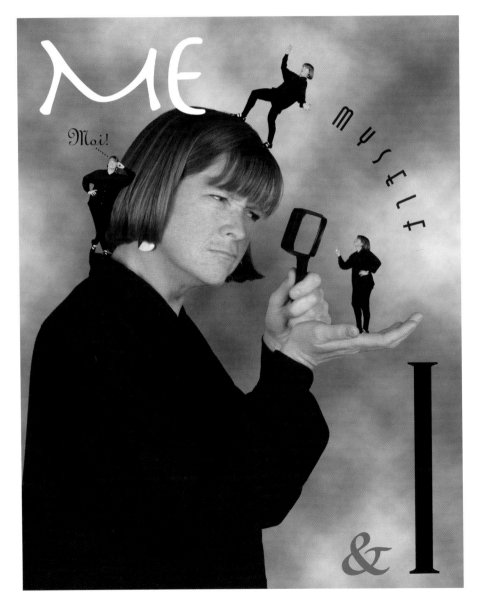

This is a simplified version of the matte technique called blue-screen composite used in the video and film industries to place a subject from one piece of film into another. Although there are many ways to do this in Adobe Photoshop, this technique will give you the most flawless results. For a blue-screen composite, the subject is photographed against a background that shares no colors with the subject. Because the subject in video is usually a person, blue or green is often the chosen background color. Before you start, analyze the colors in your subject and determine what color will be best for the background. Because you will remove the background electronically, it's important that the subject doesn't contain any of that color.

1. Photograph your subject image. For still photography, use a medium-blue backdrop that contains little to no red (a sheet of uncoated PANTONE* 279 works well). Be sure to use the same lighting direction as the background so it will fit in well. Open the subject RGB file in Adobe Photoshop.

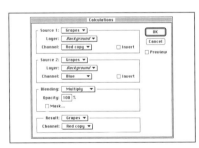

2. Now generate a matte using the red and blue channels of the image. (A matte is an image that is white in the area of the subject and black in the background.) In the Channels palette, drag the Red channel down to the New Channel icon to duplicate the channel. Select Image > Map > Invert (⌘/Ctrl+I).

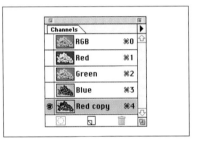

3. You create the matte by combining this new channel with the blue channel. To do this, choose Image > Calculations. Set up your Calculations dialog box like the one shown here. Multiply the blue channel by the Red copy channel, and put the result back into the Red copy channel. The Source 1 and Result filenames should be the same.

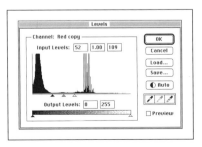

4. Adjust the densities of the matte using Levels (⌘/Ctrl+L). Drag the highlights input slider to the left of the right spike in the histogram, and drag the shadows slider to the right of the left spike. The sliders should be positioned as shown in this figure. Click OK.

5. Invert the channel (⌘/Ctrl+I). This creates a rough matte.

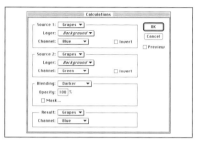

6. You now need to adjust for any partially transparent areas of the matte (such as a person's hair) that would let some of the blue-screen background show through. Choose Image > Calculations. Select the green and blue channels as the source channels and the blue channel as the result channel. Click OK.

7. Return to the RGB channel of your image. The blue areas of the image now have a green cast.

8. Load the selection mask by Option/Alt-clicking the Red copy channel in the Channels palette. If the original image had a cast shadow, there may still be shadow present in the current selection. To remove the shadow, continue with step 9. If you are satisfied with the selection, skip to step 11.

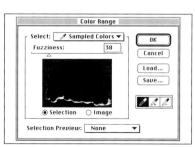

9. Deselect (⌘/Ctrl+D), and choose Select > Color Range. Make sure that Sampled Colors is selected at the top of the dialog box, and then click the shadow area that you want to remove. In this example, we sampled the cast shadow under the grapes. Shift-click additional shadow areas to add to the selection. When you have created a mask for the shadow, click OK.

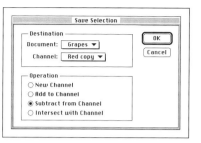

10. Choose Select > Save Selection. To remove this area from the mask you've created in the Red copy channel, select the Red copy channel in the pop-up menu and click the Subtract from Channel option. Click OK.

11. Load the new mask selection by Option/Alt-clicking the Red copy channel in the Channels palette. Then copy the image to the Clipboard, and save the file.

12. Open the background file for the composite image.

13. Paste the subject into the image. Before deselecting, make any other adjustments to integrate the subject with the background. In this example, we selected the front of the basket and then held down the Option/Alt key while choosing Edit > Paste Into to paste the subject behind the selection. We then flipped the grapes to match the background lighting.

14. Add any final touches to your composite image. In this example, we added several copies of the grapes and used the clone tool to blend them together naturally. We then used the burn tool to create shadows and to tone down highlights.

7 Printing and Production

Color trapping and overprinting

Creating duotones, tritones, and quadtones

Color trapping and overprinting

Software needed: Adobe Illustrator 4 or later

STROKE WEIGHT	TRAP IN INCHES	TRAP IN POINTS	SHAPES	LINES	TYPE
.4	.003	.2			
.6	.004	.3			
.8	.005	.4			
1.0	.007	.5			
1.5	.01	.75			
2.0	.014	1.0			
3.0	.021	1.5			

When examining printed artwork, you'll often notice registration problems in areas where two colors meet. These problems are usually caused by the paper stretching or shifting slightly on the printing press. Traditionally, color prepress operators have compensated for potential registration problems in the printed artwork by underexposing and overexposing certain areas of the film to create "trap" or "spread."

With color separation capabilities now included with many graphics programs, designers and production artists often have the option of creating trap themselves before printing film. Whether you create trap in Adobe Photoshop or Adobe Illustrator, it's important to work closely with the printer who will print the final artwork. The printer can help you locate areas in the artwork that need trap and determine how much trap they need. In addition, the printer can tell you what CMYK percentages to use to create a four-color black.

In Adobe Illustrator 5.5, you can create trap automatically using the Pathfinder Trap filter, or you can create trap manually using the Overprint option. In general, the Trap filter is recommended for trapping of simple objects, two at a time. The Trap filter does not work on placed images, type, or strokes (unless you first create outlines), and does not give good results with gradient filled objects. For trapping of objects containing placed images, text, and strokes, Adobe recommends that you use one of the manual trapping methods described in this section. For trapping of objects containing gradient fills, see page 90.

If you plan to create manual trap in your artwork, see the explanation of trap in the Adobe Illustrator User Guide before reading this section. We also recommend that you show the chart on this page to your printer to help you both determine what stroke weight will give the best results in your artwork.

How a stroked path will print

It's important to remember that the stroke straddles the path—that is, when using stroked paths to create trap, half the line weight is inside the path and the other half is outside the path. You therefore need to specify a stroke weight that is twice the amount of trap you want. For example, if you need .5-point spread trap, paint your shape with a 1-point stroke that overprints.

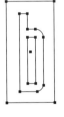

Artwork Only

Diagrammed preview
— Stroke width
— Path
— Trap

Printed piece

Using four-color blacks

If you are printing process colors, you can avoid some registration problems by using a black that contains percentages of cyan, magenta, and yellow with 100% black. In general, misregistration is less noticeable if there is at least one shared color between adjacent shapes. A four-color black is also a much richer black than 100% black alone.

100% Black

30% Cyan
100% Black

20% Cyan
15% Magenta
15% Yellow
100% Black

Overprinting colors with shared inks

If objects share common ink colors, it is not necessary to trap the colors. In this case, the common ink hides slight areas of misregistration. The Trap filter has no effect on colors with common inks.

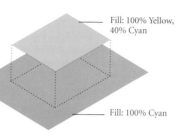

Fill: 100% Yellow, 40% Cyan

Fill: 100% Cyan

Printed result. No trap or overprint required.

Overprinting colors with no shared inks

If objects do not share common ink colors, use trap to add the overprint color to the background color where the two overlap. You can create a thin stroke and set it to overprint or use the Trap filter. Note that if you use the Trap filter, you can click the Reverse Traps option to switch between spread and choke trap.

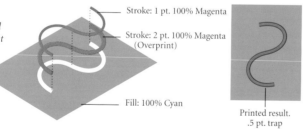

Fill: 100% Magenta

Trap: 100% Magenta 40% Cyan (Overprint)

Fill: 100% Cyan

Printed result. Overprint stroke or trap: 100% Cyan 100% Magenta

Types of trap

Trapping lines

Use when printing lines on a colored or black background. Remember that to trap type or stroked paths using the Trap filter, you must first convert the paths or type to outlines.

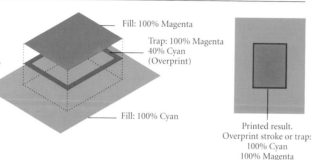

Stroke: 1 pt. 100% Magenta

Stroke: 2 pt. 100% Magenta (Overprint)

Fill: 100% Cyan

Printed result. .5 pt. trap

Black lines overprint (four-color black background)

Use when your illustration or type is reversed out of a four-color black background.

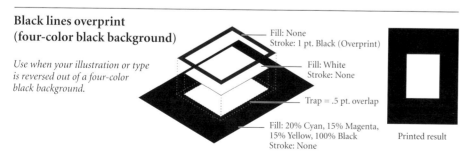

Fill: None
Stroke: 1 pt. Black (Overprint)

Fill: White
Stroke: None

Trap = .5 pt. overlap

Fill: 20% Cyan, 15% Magenta, 15% Yellow, 100% Black
Stroke: None

Printed result

Butt fit

Use when the printer provides trap electronically or photomechanically. No special preparation in Illustrator is required.

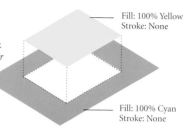

Fill: 100% Yellow
Stroke: None

Fill: 100% Cyan
Stroke: None

Printed result

Spread

Use when the background is darker than the object on top of it.

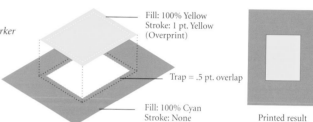

Fill: 100% Yellow
Stroke: 1 pt. Yellow (Overprint)

Trap = .5 pt. overlap

Fill: 100% Cyan
Stroke: None

Printed result

Choke

Use when the background is lighter than the object on top of it.

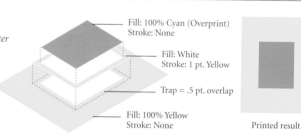

Fill: 100% Cyan (Overprint)
Stroke: None

Fill: White
Stroke: 1 pt. Yellow

Trap = .5 pt. overlap

Fill: 100% Yellow
Stroke: None

Printed result

Black lines overprint (color background)

Use when the design contains many different color tints and the illustration style allows.

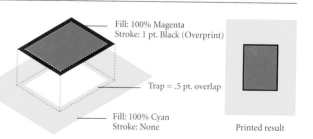

Fill: 100% Magenta
Stroke: 1 pt. Black (Overprint)

Trap = .5 pt. overlap

Fill: 100% Cyan
Stroke: None

Printed result

Using the Pathfinder Trap filter

1. Use the Pathfinder Trap filter to create automatic traps for simple artwork elements. Select two shapes at a time to trap. If you are trapping type or stroked paths, you must convert the paths or type to outlines before trapping.

2. Choose Filter > Pathfinder > Trap, and enter the thickness of the trap in points. (The example at the left has been exaggerated for visibility.) Leave the other settings at their default values unless your printer has requested other values. Repeat these steps until all elements in your artwork have been trapped. For an explanation of Trap filter options, see the Illustrator user guide.

Trapping gradients on gradients

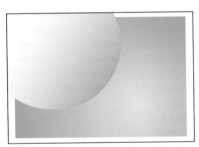

1. Gradient fills with no common colors are especially difficult to trap. Before you begin, it's important to first consult with your prepress vendor to determine which gradient will hold the trap. Then open a copy of the file, and select both objects. Copy them to the Clipboard, and choose File > Paste In Front (⌘F). Deselect.

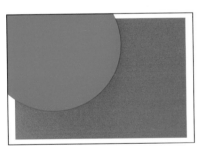

2. Select the copy of the object that will hold the trap (in this example, the green background object), and fill it with 100% magenta. We will call this object the primary object. Then select the copy of the second object, and fill it with 100% cyan. These flat-color fills will be used to create the trap.

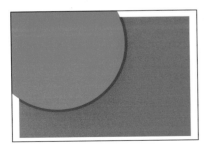

3. Select both flat-color objects, and choose Filter > Pathfinder > Trap. The resulting shape is your trap. (The example at the left has been exaggerated for visibility.) The trap overlays the magenta copy of the primary object.

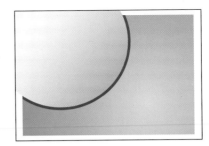

4. Select just the two flat-color objects and delete them. The two gradient-filled objects and the trap object should remain. (The Trap filter automatically sets the trap object to Overprint.)

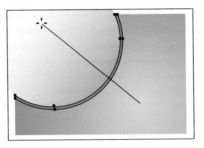

5. Now you will create a gradient with colors common to both gradients to fill the trap object. Open the Gradient dialog box. Select the gradient used in the primary object, and click Duplicate.

6. Select just the trap object, and fill it with the copy of the gradient fill you just created. Then select the gradient fill tool. Position the pointer at the beginning of the gradient fill within the primary object (if the fill is radial, position the pointer at the center of the fill) and drag across the trap object. This aligns the two gradient fills.

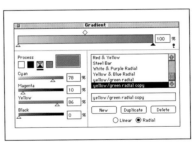

7. Now adjust the colors of the gradient fill within the trap object so that it blends into the objects being trapped. To do this, add some color from the non-primary gradient fill to the copy of the gradient fill. In this example, we added magenta to both ends of the copy to make the trap object blend better with the yellow and green background.

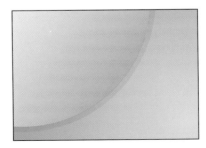

8. If necessary, zoom in on the artwork so that you can better see the results of your adjustments. When the trap object blends with both surrounding gradients, save the file.

Creating duotones, tritones, and quadtones

Software needed: Adobe Photoshop 2.5 or later

Adobe Photoshop provides the ability to create monotones, duotones, tritones, and quad-tones. Monotones are grayscale images printed with a single, non-black ink. Duotones, tritones, and quadtones are grayscale images printed with two, three, and four inks, respectively. In these images, the colored inks are used to reproduce different tonal values rather than different colors.

Duotones, tritones, and quadtones have been used for years by designers to increase the tonal range of black-and-white photographs. Although a black-and-white photographic reproduction can reproduce up to 256 levels of gray, a single plate on a printing press can reproduce only about 50 levels of gray. The use of two, three, or four inks to print a black-and-white photograph, therefore, significantly increases the number of gray levels that can be reproduced. The results are a dramatic improvement in the reproduction of subtle detail and in the overall quality of the image.

A typical duotone uses a black ink to capture the shadow detail in an image and a gray or colored ink for the midtone and highlight areas. In Adobe Photoshop, you specify how each ink is distributed across the shadow and highlight areas of the image using the Duotone Curve dialog box. This dialog box displays a curve, similar to the transfer function used by Photoshop to compensate for dot gain or loss by the imagesetter. The duotone transfer curve maps each grayscale value on the original image to the actual ink percentage that will be used to print the image. So, for example, if you enter 70 in the 100% text box, a 70% dot of that ink color will be used to print the 100% shadow areas of the image. Keep in mind that you specify a duotone curve for each of the inks used to print a duotone, tritone, or quadtone image.

The following pages show some examples of duotones, tritones, and quadtones created in Adobe Photoshop using Pantone® black and various shades of gray or color. The duotone curves used to determine the distribution of each ink were created by specifying only three to six points on the curve. Although the Duotone Curve function lets you specify up to 13 points on the graph, if you specify fewer points, Photoshop automatically calculates the intermediate values.

Each of the examples shown here also includes the overprint colors specified in Adobe Photoshop for the image. The Overprint Colors feature lets you tell Photoshop exactly what colors result when the various combinations of inks are overlayed so that the program can accurately display the image. To do this, you simply select the color you want to change in the Overprint Colors dialog box and adjust the color values until the color looks as it should. Note that this adjustment affects only your screen display and not your final output.

A final consideration when creating duotones is that both the order in which the inks are printed and the screen angles you use have a dramatic effect on your final output. In general, to ensure the most fully saturated colors, darker inks should be printed before lighter inks. If you're using Photoshop to set the screen angles, use the Auto button in the Halftone Screens dialog box. If your output device is equipped with PostScript Level 2, be sure to also select the Accurate Screens option. Note that if you're using an electronic prepress system, such as a Scitex®, Photoshop's screen settings are ignored. In this case, work with your service bureau or prepress operator to set the screen angle.

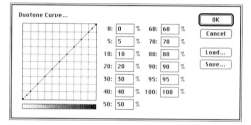

The Duotone Curve dialog box allows you to specify the distribution of each ink by specifying density (i.e., dot size) adjustments for up to 13 points on the curve. The curve shown here is a linear curve, where each grayscale value from the original image is mapped to the same density value of the given ink. This means that a 10% gray on the original image will be printed with a 10% density value of the given ink, a 90% gray will be printed with a 90% density of the ink, and so on.

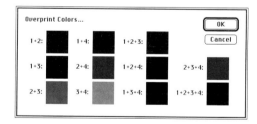

To make sure that Photoshop accurately displays overprint colors on-screen, select the overprint color you want to modify and then adjust the color values until the color appears correct. If possible, use a printed sample of the overprinted inks to ensure the most accurate screen display. Before adjusting colors on-screen, it is important that you have accurately calibrated your system according to the instructions in the Photoshop user guide.

Duotones

Printing specifications:
175-line screen / 2400-dpi imagesetter

Screen angles:
Ink 1: 45°   Ink 2: 15°

Printing Inks:

Ink 1:
Black

Ink 2:
PMS Cool Gray 10

Overprint Color:

Ink 1+2

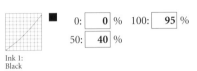

0: [0] %   100: [95] %
50: [40] %

Ink 1:
Black

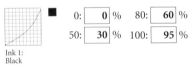

0: [0.5] %   100: [70] %
50: [20] %

Ink 2:
PMS Cool Gray 10

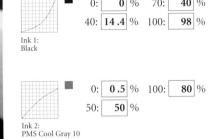

0: [0] %   70: [40] %
40: [14.4] %   100: [98] %

Ink 1:
Black

0: [0.5] %   100: [80] %
50: [50] %

Ink 2:
PMS Cool Gray 10

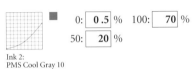

0: [0] %   80: [60] %
50: [30] %   100: [95] %

Ink 1:
Black

0: [0.5] %   100: [95] %
50: [40] %

Ink 2:
PMS Cool Gray 10

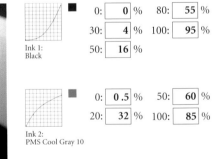

0: [0] %   80: [55] %
30: [4] %   100: [95] %
50: [16] %

Ink 1:
Black

0: [0.5] %   50: [60] %
20: [32] %   100: [85] %

Ink 2:
PMS Cool Gray 10

Duotones

Printing specifications:
175-line screen / 2400-dpi imagesetter

Screen angles:
Ink 1: 45°   Ink 2: 15°

Printing Inks:

Ink 1:
Black

Ink 2:
PMS 485

Overprint Color:

Ink 1+2

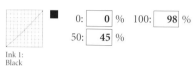

Ink 1:
Black

0: [0] %   100: [98] %
50: [45] %

Ink 2:
PMS 485

0: [0.5] %   100: [55] %
50: [15] %

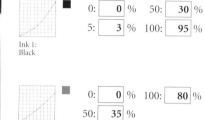

Ink 1:
Black

0: [0] %   50: [30] %
5: [3] %   100: [95] %

Ink 2:
PMS 485

0: [0] %   100: [80] %
50: [35] %

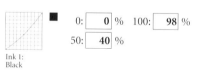

Ink 1:
Black

0: [0] %   100: [98] %
50: [40] %

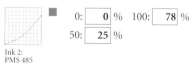

Ink 2:
PMS 485

0: [0] %   100: [78] %
50: [25] %

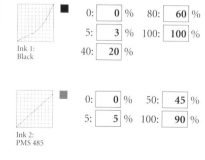

Ink 1:
Black

0: [0] %   80: [60] %
5: [3] %   100: [100] %
40: [20] %

Ink 2:
PMS 485

0: [0] %   50: [45] %
5: [5] %   100: [90] %

Tritones

Printing specifications:
175-line screen / 2400-dpi imagesetter

Screen angles:
Ink 1: 45°   Ink 2: 15°   Ink 3: 75°

Printing Inks:

Ink 1:
Black

Ink 2:
PMS Cool Gray 10

Ink 3:
PMS Cool Gray 1

Overprint Colors:

Ink 1+2   Ink 1+3   Ink 2+3   Ink 1+2+3

SOFT

Ink 1:
Black

| 0: | 0 | % | 80: | 40 | % |
| 50: | 5 | % | 100: | 100 | % |

Ink 2:
PMS Cool Gray 10

| 0: | 0 | % | 50: | 30.5 | % |
| 20: | 12 | % | 100: | 95 | % |

Ink 3:
PMS Cool Gray 1

| 0: | 0 | % | 100: | 100 | % |
| 40: | 73.8 | % | | | |

NORMAL

Ink 1:
Black

0:	0	%	80:	40	%
30:	5	%	90:	67	%
50:	10	%	100:	100	%

Ink 2:
PMS Cool Gray 10

| 0: | 0 | % | 100: | 95 | % |
| 50: | 45 | % | | | |

Ink 3:
PMS Cool Gray 1

| 0: | 0 | % | 100: | 100 | % |
| 40: | 74 | % | | | |

LOW CONTRAST

Ink 1:
Black

| 0: | 0 | % | 50: | 10 | % |
| 30: | 2 | % | 100: | 70 | % |

Ink 2:
PMS Cool Gray 10

| 0: | 5 | % | 100: | 80 | % |
| 50: | 20 | % | | | |

Ink 3:
PMS Cool Gray 1

| 0: | 10 | % | 100: | 100 | % |
| 50: | 80 | % | | | |

DARK

Ink 1:
Black

0:	0	%	80:	60	%
30:	5	%	90:	80	%
50:	20	%	100:	100	%

Ink 2:
PMS Cool Gray 10

| 0: | 0 | % | 100: | 95 | % |
| 50: | 40 | % | | | |

Ink 3:
PMS Cool Gray 1

| 0: | 0 | % | 100: | 100 | % |
| 40: | 74 | % | | | |

Quadtones

Printing specifications:
175-line screen / 2400-dpi imagesetter

Screen angles:
Ink 1: 45°   Ink 2: 15°   Ink 3: 75°   Ink 4: 0°

Printing Inks:

Ink 1:
Black

Ink 2:
PMS Cool Gray 10

Ink 3:
PMS Cool Gray 4

Ink 4:
PMS Cool Gray 1

Overprint Colors:

Ink 1+2   Ink 1+3   Ink 2+3   Ink 1+4   Ink 2+4   Ink 3+4

Ink 1+2+3   Ink 1+2+4   Ink 1+3+4   Ink 2+3+4   Ink 1+2+3+4

SOFT

   0: 0 %   80: 35 %
50: 5 %   100: 100 %

Ink 1:
Black

   0: 0 %   100: 80 %
50: 20 %

Ink 2:
PMS Cool Gray 10

   0: 0 %   100: 85 %
40: 40 %

Ink 3:
PMS Cool Gray 4

   0: 0 %   100: 100 %
50: 50 %

Ink 4:
PMS Cool Gray 1

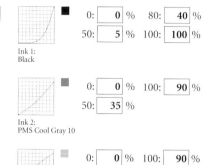

NORMAL

0: 0 %   80: 40 %
50: 5 %   100: 100 %

Ink 1:
Black

0: 0 %   100: 90 %
50: 35 %

Ink 2:
PMS Cool Gray 10

0: 0 %   100: 90 %
40: 45 %

Ink 3:
PMS Cool Gray 4

0: 0 %   50: 70 %
5: 10 %   100: 100 %

Ink 4:
PMS Cool Gray 1

LOW CONTRAST

   0: 0 %   50: 10 %
30: 2 %   100: 65 %

Ink 1:
Black

   0: 5 %   100: 70 %
50: 20 %

Ink 2:
PMS Cool Gray 10

   0: 10 %   100: 70 %
40: 25 %

Ink 3:
PMS Cool Gray 4

0: 10 %   100: 100 %
50: 80 %

Ink 4:
PMS Cool Gray 1

DARK

0: 0 %   80: 40 %
50: 5 %   100: 100 %

Ink 1:
Black

0: 0 %   100: 90 %
50: 45 %

Ink 2:
PMS Cool Gray 10

0: 0 %   100: 90 %
40: 60 %

Ink 3:
PMS Cool Gray 4

0: 0 %   50: 80 %
5: 10 %   100: 100 %

Ink 4:
PMS Cool Gray 1

Quadtones

Printing specifications:
175-line screen / 2400-dpi imagesetter

Screen angles:
Ink 1: 45°   Ink 2: 15°   Ink 3: 75°   Ink 4: 0°

Printing Inks:

Ink 1:
Black

Ink 2:
PMS 485

Ink 3:
PMS Cool Gray 4

Ink 4:
PMS Cool Gray 1

Overprint Colors:

Ink 1+2   Ink 1+3   Ink 2+3   Ink 1+4   Ink 2+4   Ink 3+4

Ink 1+2+3   Ink 1+2+4   Ink 1+3+4   Ink 2+3+4   Ink 1+2+3+4

Ink			
Ink 1: Black	0: 0 %	80: 45 %	
	50: 10 %	100: 100 %	
Ink 2: PMS 485	0: 0 %	70: 25 %	
	30: 5 %	100: 60 %	
Ink 3: PMS Cool Gray 4	0: 0 %	100: 100 %	
	40: 65 %		
Ink 4: PMS Cool Gray 1	0: 0 %	50: 80 %	
	5: 5 %	100: 100 %	

Ink			
Ink 1: Black	0: 0 %	80: 40 %	
	50: 8 %	100: 100 %	
Ink 2: PMS 485	0: 0 %	70: 38 %	
	30: 9 %	100: 80 %	
Ink 3: PMS Cool Gray 4	0: 0 %	100: 100 %	
	40: 60 %		
Ink 4: PMS Cool Gray 1	0: 0 %	50: 80 %	
	5: 10 %	100: 100 %	

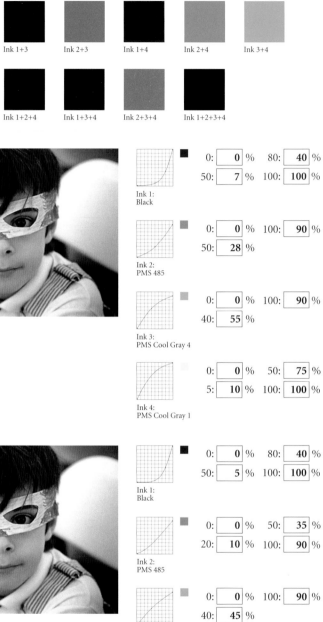

Ink			
Ink 1: Black	0: 0 %	80: 40 %	
	50: 7 %	100: 100 %	
Ink 2: PMS 485	0: 0 %	100: 90 %	
	50: 28 %		
Ink 3: PMS Cool Gray 4	0: 0 %	100: 90 %	
	40: 55 %		
Ink 4: PMS Cool Gray 1	0: 0 %	50: 75 %	
	5: 10 %	100: 100 %	

Ink			
Ink 1: Black	0: 0 %	80: 40 %	
	50: 5 %	100: 100 %	
Ink 2: PMS 485	0: 0 %	50: 35 %	
	20: 10 %	100: 90 %	
Ink 3: PMS Cool Gray 4	0: 0 %	100: 90 %	
	40: 45 %		
Ink 4: PMS Cool Gray 1	0: 0 %	50: 70 %	
	5: 10 %	100: 100 %	

Bibliography

ABES, CATHY. *Photoshop f/x.*
Chapel Hill, NC.: Ventana Press, Inc., 1994.

ADOBE SYSTEMS, INC. *Beyond the Basics: Adobe Illustrator Version 5.5.*
Mountain View, CA: 1994.

———. *Beyond the Basics: Adobe Photoshop Version 3.0.*
Mountain View, CA: 1994.

———. *Classroom in a Book: Adobe Illustrator.*
Mountain View, CA: Adobe Press/Hayden Books, 1994.

———. *Classroom in a Book: Adobe Photoshop, Second Edition.*
Mountain View, CA: Adobe Press/Hayden Books, 1994.

———. *Classroom in a Book: Advanced Adobe Photoshop.*
Mountain View, CA: Adobe Press/Hayden Books, 1994.

ANDRES, CLAY. *Illustrator Illuminated.*
Berkeley, CA: Peachpit Press Inc., 1992.

ALSPACH, TED. *Macworld Illustrator 5.0/5.5 Bible.*
San Mateo, CA: IDG Books Worldwide, Inc. 1994.

BIEDNY, DAVID, BERT MONROY, AND MARK SIPRUT. *The Official Photoshop Handbook, 2.5 Edition.* New York: Bantam Books, 1993.

BRINGHURST, ROBERT. *The Elements of Typographic Style.*
Point Roberts, WA: Hartley and Marks, 1992.

BRUNO, MICHAEL. *Pocket Pal,* 15th Edition.
New York: International Paper Company, 1992.

COHEN, LUANNE, RUSSELL BROWN, AND TANYA WENDLING. *Imaging Essentials.*
Mountain View, CA: Adobe Press/Hayden Books, 1993.

DAY, ROB. *Designer Photoshop.*
New York: Random House, 1993.

DATON, LINNEA, AND JACK DAVIS. *The Photoshop WOW Book.*
Berkely, CA: Peachpit Press, Inc., 1993.

ENDO, ETSURO. *Adobe Photoshop A to Z.*
Tokyo: Bug News Network, 1993.

FIELD, GARY G. *Color and Its Reproduction.*
Pittsburgh, PA: Graphic Arts Technical Foundation, 1988.

GREENBERG, ADELE DROBLAS, AND SETH GREENBERG. *Fundamental Photoshop.*
Berkeley, CA: Osborne McGraw Hill, 1994.

IGARASHI, TAKENOBU, AND DIANE BURNS. *Designers on Mac.*
Tokyo: Graphic-sha Publishing Company, 1992.

LAWLER, BRIAN. *The Color Resource Complete Guide to Trapping.*
San Francisco: The Color Resource, 1993.

MCCLELLAND, DEKE. *Macworld Photoshop 3 Bible, 2nd Edition.*
Foster City, CA: IDG Books Worldwide, Inc., 1994.

———. *The Illustrator 5.0/5.5 Book.*
Berkeley, CA: Peachpit Press, Inc., 1994.

MILLER, MARC D. AND RANDY ZAUCHA. *The Color Mac.*
Carmel, IN: Hayden Books, 1992.

NIFFENEGGER, BILL. *Photoshop Filter Finesse.*
 New York: Random House, Inc., 1994.

RICH, JIM, AND SANDY BOZEK. *Photoshop in Black and White.*
 Berkeley, CA: Peachpit Press, 1994.

SOUTHWORTH, MILES, THAD MCILROY, AND DONNA SOUTHWORTH.
 The Color Resource Complete Color Glossary.
 San Francisco: The Color Resource, 1992.

SPIEKERMANN, ERIK, AND E. M. GINGER. *Stop Stealing Sheep & Find Out How Type Works.*
 Mountain View, CA: Adobe Press/Hayden Books, 1993.

STEUER, SHARON. *The Illustrator WOW Book.*
 Berkeley, CA: Peachpit Press, Inc., 1995.

TAPSCOTT, DIANE, LISA JEANS, AND PAT SOBERANIS. *Production Essentials.*
 Mountain View, CA: Adobe Press/Hayden Books, 1994.

WEINMANN, ELAINE, AND PETER LOUREKAS. *Illustrator 5.5 for Macintosh.*
 Berkeley, CA: Peachpit Press, Inc, 1994.

WILLIAMS, ROBIN. *How to Boss Your Fonts Around.*
 Berkeley, CA: Peachpit Press, 1994.

WILLIAMS, ROBIN. *The Mac Is Not a Typewriter.*
 Berkeley, CA: Peachpit Press, 1990.

Index

Colophon

This book was designed and produced using Adobe Illustrator, Adobe Photoshop, Adobe Type Manager, and QuarkXPress on the Power Macintosh 8100/80. The Adobe Original Minion™ and Minion Expert typefaces are used throughout the book.

Final film was printed at 150 lines per inch on an Adobe/Scitex RIP with a PixelBurst™ coprocessor using Adobe Accurate Screens™ and a Scitex Dolev™ imagesetter by Metagraphics, Palo Alto, California. Final film for the duotone, tritone, and quadtone section was printed at 175 lines per inch.

The book was printed by Shepard Poorman, Indianapolis, Indiana.